SEASONS WITH THE KESTREL

SEASONS WITH THE KESTREL

GORDON RIDDLE

BLANDFORD

For Rosie, Keith and Gael

Blandford
An imprint of Cassell,
Villiers House, 41/47 Strand, London WC2N 5JE

First published in the UK 1992

Distributed in Australia by
Capricorn Link (Australia) Pty Ltd
P.O. Box 665, Lane Cove, NSW 2066

British Library Cataloguing in Publication Data
Riddle, Gordon
  Seasons with the kestrel.
  1. Kestrels
  1. Title
  598.91

ISBN 0-7137-2243-6

Typeset by Chapterhouse, The Cloisters, Halsall Lane Formby, L37 3PX

Printed and bound in Singapore by Kyodo Printing Co.

CONTENTS

Imperial/Metric Conversions

1 mm	=	0.0394 in
1 cm	=	0.394 in
10 cm	=	3.94 in
1 m	=	3.281 ft
1,000 m	=	3,281 ft
1 km	=	0.621 miles
10 km	=	6.21 miles
1 g	=	0.035 oz
10 g	=	0.35 oz
100 g	=	3.5 oz

ACKNOWLEDGEMENTS

I have thoroughly enjoyed working with the kestrel over the past 18 years in Ayrshire and one of the greatest pleasures has been meeting so many people who shared my enthusiasm. Early tentative contacts have resulted in firm friendships. They are a hardy breed, willing to scour the hillsides in all weather to track down the often elusive kestrel. Their enthusiasm, dedication and unfailing optimism have been a great strength. They will undoubtedly appreciate more than anyone else the ups and downs related in this book. Without them this study, and therefore the book, would still be a pipe dream.

My sincere thanks go to Bill Brackenridge, John Burlieson, John and Jean Burton, David Callan, the two Duncan Camerons and Sam Cameron, Alex Connell, Tommy and Gerrard Connolly, Hugh Gibson, Dick Gladwell, John Gray, Robin Heaney, Angus Hogg, Ian Hopkins, Alistair Kerr, Iain Leach, Jessie and Meikle McKay, Bill McKechnie, Lea MacNally, Richard Mearns, John Melrose, George Morrison, Charlie Park, John Rhead, Kevin Roberts, Chris Rollie, Alan Ross, Dick Roxburgh, Carol Scott, Wallace Simpson, Don and Annie Smith, Andy Village, Donald Watson, Matthew Wilson, John Wykes, Bernie Zonfrillo and all those who have helped in some way. With the passage of time some helpers are no longer with us: Graham Stewart, Jim Murdoch, Jim Fulton, Fred Hutcheson and John Phillips.

The Ranger Team at Culzean Country Park, Deirdre Mackinnon, Mike Callan, Lorna Cawood, Stephen Wiseman and seasonal staff have been particularly supportive, backing me up on innumerable field outings or covering back at base. Mike and Deirdre, in particular, have spent an enormous amount of time up trees, acting as 'anchor persons' on the rope and never dreaming of promotion, patiently confirming occupation of territories or pinpointing nest sites. Deirdre drew the figures and has done more to advance the work than any other helper and my special thanks go to her.

Landowners have been extremely co-operative in permitting access to kestrel breeding territories and allowing nest boxes to be erected. Staff of the Forestry Commission, Economic Forestry Group, Fountain Forestry, Imperial

7

Chemical Industries and Scottish Power have shown a great interest in the work as have many estate owners and farmers, such as James Murdoch and his family and the Eccles family.

Generous grants were received from the Scottish Ornithologists Club; licences were provided by the Nature Conservancy Council; and data was made available by the British Trust for Ornithology. The members of the South-west Scottish Raptor Group have provided a welcome forum for discussion under the auspices of Dave Dick (Royal Society for the Protection of Birds) and the irrepressible Dick Roxburgh. Analysis of kestrel casualties was undertaken by Dr Ruthven at the Department of Agriculture and Fisheries for Scotland at East Craigs, Edinburgh. Sheena Andrew at the Carnegie Library, Ayr, and Bill Harper at the Waterson Library, Edinburgh, were extremely helpful with the background research work.

Wendy Hollingworth, Rosemary Riddle and Alison McCutcheon typed the first manuscripts and tackled the formidable task of interpreting my scrawl and spelling. Wendy did a superb job producing the final copy on a word processor. Dr Jack Jackson, Sheilah Jackson, Deirdre Mackinnon, Bette Meek, Margaret Johnstone and Margaret Watt gave up their valuable time to read through the first draft and make many constructive comments.

Last, but no means least, I would like to thank my family who have shown great interest in the work. Keith and Gael, my children, have spent a lot of 'days out' near kestrel sites which I just happened to check while we were there and Rosie, my wife, has been a kestrel widow on many occasions. The hours spent with Keith in the hills, as he has developed skills, will be memories never forgotten. This book is dedicated to them, as they have worked just as hard in their own ways in order to make it possible.

Gordon Riddle
Culzean

INTRODUCTORY NOTE

*T*he charismatic appeal of birds of prey is easily explained in terms of their beauty, historical links with man, the wild nature of their lifestyle and the places they haunt. The kestrel needs little introduction even to the layman. It is a bird of the open countryside, rarely penetrating the close confines of dense woodland exploited by the sparrowhawk. The kestrel is most often recognised because it hovers when hunting.

Though not as spectacular as the golden eagle, osprey or peregrine falcon, this compact, medium-sized raptor has the distinction of being described as common, a feat in itself in the fluctuating world of predatory birds. The kestrel has flourished while many of its close relatives have marked time or declined.

HOOKED

Diary extract – June 1988:

I gingerly flexed one leg, then the other. Blood began to flow into cramped muscles and the prospect of exiting the hide and climbing down the tree did not appeal. Five hours had elapsed since I'd settled down opposite the nest box, full of anticipation, notebook and camera at the ready. The huddle of dozing kestrel chicks, a full hatch of six, had only been fed once during the intervening period, much to our mutual disappointment. The immaculate cock bird had flown in quickly with no warning and deposited a decapitated meadow pipit at the feet of the startled chicks. Not even pausing to watch the ensuing mêlée as his progeny jostled for possession of the prey item, he departed as quickly and silently as he'd arrived. Eight seconds out of 18,000, three photographs and another snippet of information stored away in the files.

There have been thousands of such incidents over the last quarter century since I became hooked on one very special bird of prey – the kestrel. It all began by chance. When school holidays came around I could usually be found at Horncliffe, a small village several miles upriver from the Tweed Estuary. Each day the number of cormorants was studiously counted as they roosted on the topmost branches of the beeches by the river-bank. These long-suffering trees were whitewashed by generations of these black fishermen. The wooded slopes continually needed exploring and the glens always held a challenge.

One bleak December morning I was trudging up a favourite glen, making for the ruined mill and the possibility of dipper or grey wagtail, when all hell let loose. The peaceful scene of redpolls dangling from alders and blackbirds foraging among leaf litter was shattered as a cock kestrel burst over the tree line and scattered a flock of skylarks.

From the dozen birds one unfortunate individual was singled out and forced to dive earthwards twisting and calling out in panic. The stand of blackthorn bushes by the burn offered refuge but the determined kestrel ignored the barbs and plunged in, talons outstretched. Out came the lark, out came the kestrel, in went the lark, in went the kestrel. In desperation the terrified bird tried to gain deeper cover, caught a wing and careered into the banking.

The kestrel lost no time in despatching the bird only then noticing my presence not three metres away. Predictably, the glare was brief and the departure, heavily laden, was swift. The year was 1963, I was 16 and the seed of interest was well and truly sown.

It wasn't just the dramatic nature of the incident that intrigued me but the unconventional method of attack and choice of prey. There was obviously more to the kestrel than just hovering.

The next location of note was an elm tree in Sunlaws Estate near Kelso. I can still picture clearly the hen kestrel sunning herself at the edge of the nest hole and remember the thrill of seeing five white bundles huddled among the debris of a recently plucked song thrush. Each beak was tinged with red from the feast and I caught for the first time the characteristic whiff of kestrel. Hearing that the brood was under the death sentence from the local gamekeeper, a friend, Chris Dickson, removed three of the young just in time. At least they were given a chance. Lessons were being learned.

I became an avid collector of kestrel pellets which were carefully dissected to reveal fragments of bone, feather and beetle legs – all clues to the varied diet of the bird. I also became familiar with a pair of kestrels in an estate nearer my home. Their choice of nest site was in a line of mature beeches in the middle of a jackdaw colony. Life wasn't easy for the pair which suffered intense mobbing as well as fierce competition for the actual site – a huge gash in the trunk of an ancient hardwood.

Attempts to climb the tree were unsuccessful due to the smooth bark and lack of handholds. The solution involved smuggling a double ladder from the house to the nest site, a mere mile, but the reward of the close encounter with a two-week-old youngster made the effort worthwhile. Two unhatched eggs, partly buried among the fragmented pellets were removed for analysis but only after the back of my hand had been raked in classic kestrel fashion. The entrance was littered with twigs, ample evidence of jackdaw's persistent attempts to build a nest on the same site. Many times I was able to approach the nest and watch the adults flying in with food or see the young kestrel napping in the July sunshine. Then one day three kestrels were flying above the fields and within a week stock doves were in residence.

Since my dramatic initiation into the world of birds of prey, I've enjoyed many hours in search of and in the company of kestrels. The more I learn the more I realise just how little we know of this absorbing falcon. The easiest way to make a fool of yourself is to generalise about some aspect of the kestrel's life. However it was only when I moved to Ayrshire in 1972 to take up a ranger post at Culzean Country Park that I systematically began to study the kestrel. Springs and summers would never be the same again.

THE AYRSHIRE SCENE

My work on the kestrel in Ayrshire began soon after I arrived at Culzean, courtesy of a Ranger Naturalist guided walk which I was leading on the coastline. We stopped for a picnic lunch near a large cliff and a cursory sweep with the binoculars picked up the tell-tale white droppings below a hole in the dense ivy-clad face. Four down-covered heads were peering down at the intruders. The site was christened the Coastal Cliff and it became the first pin on the map of the district and the first piece of data in the card index system. Thus stimulated, I sat down and began to plan the campaign.

High on the agenda was to get some idea of the past status of the bird in the county. The library was an obvious starting point and consequently the local ornithological literature of the last 100 years was scrutinised for any mention of the kestrel. The unanimous assessment was that the kestrel was common, but no quantitative details were available. It was a case of starting from scratch. The locations of half a dozen sites were gleaned from the books plus odd snippets of information which gave a fascinating insight into old attitudes and practices. For example, the report of an outing on 11 June 1898 (published in the *Annals of the Kilmarnock Glenfield Ramblers Society,* 1897–1901) contained the following passage:

> On the way downhill a kestrel darted out from a cleft in the precipitous face of the hill where its nest was securely built...Mr Hastings told us about finding in a tree a nest of this species containing 4 young kestrels. He took 3 of the young birds home with him, and on visiting the nest sometime afterwards found that the assiduous parents had brought to the nest 3 young grouse and 2 young pheasants for food to the only member of their family that had been spared. Still the kestrel is a handsome bird, and ought to be protected by law on account of the benefit it certainly confers on agriculture, though it does sometimes vary its diet of mice with a few young grouse or pheasants.

Another author reported the custom of killing an old horse in winter in order to feed the retrievers. The carcass was hung up in sections on a beech tree and on several occasions merlins and kestrels were flushed from the feast.

One very revealing local statement highlights the attitude towards birds of prey in the nineteenth century, which eventually led to many species being reduced in range and others exterminated. In 1808 the Marquis of Bute, who was proposing to set up a sporting estate on the island, posted his intent by writing to other local lairds outlining his proposals. This included the employment of gamekeepers, the stocking and release of pheasants and the destruction of vermin which he claimed would prevent the birds flourishing. A form of agreement which the keepers were expected to swear under oath was enclosed and the final paragraph left nothing to the imagination...

And finally that I shall use my best endeavours to destroy all Birds of Prey, etc. with their nests, etc., whenever they can be found therein.
So help me God.

A bounty list for birds of prey, their eggs and young was appended.

EARLY HISTORY – BEFORE THE GUN

Tracing the history of the kestrel from early records to the present day reveals a chequered relationship between man and birds of prey in this country. It is obviously difficult to evaluate the status of the kestrel pre-1800 but once the battle lines were drawn up between man and birds of prey following the advent of the gun and game preservation, documentation is reasonably accurate.

The first record of the kestrel comes from Ireland in the form of a late Iron Age fossil found in the company of bear, giant deer and coot at Ballynamintra Cave near Cappagh in County Waterford. This is probably as good a point as any to begin the story as the first inroads were being made by man into a heavily forested Britain which must have favoured sparrowhawks and goshawks rather than birds of the open country like the kestrel.

Allied to the Irish records details of potential prey items for the kestrel, such as field voles and field mice, featured in the lists of remains at Iron Age Glastonbury.

Man as a hunter probably had little impact on raptor populations but the small-scale clearing of the forests by early farmers must have given the kestrel a vital new opening. Although the hovering kestrel was probably a rare sight for these early pioneers the situation was to change dramatically as successive generations reduced Britain's forest mantle at an alarming rate.

The opening up of the landscape and the emergence of sheep rearing on a huge scale must have provided ideal habitats and prey populations for the kestrel. By the eleventh century Britain's original 16 million hectares of forest had been reduced to about 4 million hectares and by the middle of the thirteenth century there were approximately eight million sheep in Britain, outnumbering the human population by more than two to one. The vast sheep walks created in the south of Scotland by the Cistercian monks, patronised by David I, and the large populations of small mammals associated with them, must have suited the kestrel.

Deforestation continued unabated through medieval times in parallel with a measure of protection for birds of prey due to the popularity of falconry between the twelfth and the seventeenth centuries. This protection, which was accompanied by severe penalites for those who dared abuse the system, was geared to the more spectacular raptor species such as the peregrine, goshawk and merlin, rather than the kestrel. The hunting prowess of the peregrine, for example, was reflected in the high prices paid by the nobility for good specimens. The light, but dynamic, merlin was a favourite of the ladies and Mary, Queen of Scots, was a keen exponent of the aerial chase.

The type of wild quarry taken by the kestrel meant that its status in falconry circles, as recorded in the *Boke of St Albans* (fifteenth century), was firmly at the foot of the table. In spite of this, the kestrel was probably used to give aspiring young falconers, in the lower echelons of society, valuable experience in managing a bird of prey. The Revd. C. A. Johns in his book *British Birds and their Haunts* quotes: 'The Kestrel was formerly trained to hunt small birds and in the court of Louis XIII was taught to hawk for bats', which suggests that some people at least persevered with the kestrel as a trained falcon.

It is probably reasonable to assume that the kestrel population did not suffer too badly in medieval times from falconry pressures but this demanding sport gave way to the gun. Within a hundred years a revolution took place in shooting techniques. The crossbow was replaced in turn by the flintlock and breach-loader, and the sporting estate was spawned. Enclosure of the land also meant a great reduction in the availability of good hawking ground and falconry became very elitist. Clubs were set up with high subscription rates which excluded the ordinary man.

Thus began a new era in the relationship between man and raptors, when the respect, admiration and care levelled by falconers was replaced by a very different set of values. Words like gibbet, vermin, pole traps, baiting and poison are synonymous with this period of slaughter which was as senseless as it was comprehensive.

Cock kestrel with field vole prey.

PERSECUTION AND POISON

The lack of information on the kestrel's status changed after 1800 with the onset of game rearing for sporting purposes. Figures from game records paint a bleak picture. The kestrel, though it probably escaped the worst excesses of persecution of birds of prey by the gamekeeping fraternity, was by no means immune. Any keeper worth his salt could not fail to note the negligible effect which the kestrel had on game rearing interests, but the bounty system was all-embracing and anything with a hooked beak and talons was fair game. If his income was increased by killing kestrels and enhancing his line of bodies hung on the gibbets to impress the laird, then you can only blame the system and his superiors who introduced it.

Remarkably, in the face of all the persecution, the kestrel entered the twentieth century on a high note when the response of kestrels to the vole plagues in the Scottish Borders resulted in good publicity for the 'beneficial' bird. Nationwide the kestrel population was never really in danger of reaching perilously low levels and during the two World Wars the absence of gamekeepers on the ground, due to their serving in the Armed Forces, meant that birds of prey enjoyed a respite.

The use of organochlorine pesticides in the post-war years was seen as a panacea to the problem of insect pests affecting agricultural crops. Many of the chemicals, as well as being extremely toxic, had the deadly quality of being persistent in the environment, passing up the various levels in the food chains, finally to accumulate in lethal doses at the predator level. Numerous incidents in the late 1950s of bird deaths in Britain caused alarm and initiated research both into the reason for mortality and into the current status of many birds of prey.

The picture which emerged was one of swift catastrophic population crashes mainly in species like the sparrowhawk and peregrine which preyed extensively on grain-eating finches and pigeons. The kestrel was far from immune and from 1953 to 1963 there had been a serious decline in populations in eastern and south-eastern England. The decline became less marked towards the south-west of Britain and to the north, and did not appear to affect the north-west of England or Scotland as badly as elsewhere. Nationally, analysis of dead raptors was undertaken in parallel with the population studies and the work revealed lethal levels of toxic chemicals in the tissues of the kestrel as well as other species. Small mammals feeding on arable fields were just as likely to ingest pesticide residues as invertebrates and birds, and, as the kestrel's diet is fairly catholic, intake of chemicals in this type of habitat was inevitable.

Despite the fact that much of the evidence was circumstantial and that surveys were by no means totally comprehensive, the pressure mounted to reduce the widespread use of certain chemicals. As voluntary, then legal bans reduced the use of these pesticides, so the kestrel mounted a recovery once more.

Between 1968 and 1978, the kestrel population in Britain increased five fold and since then it has fluctuated within relatively narrow limits. Major changes in land use, like the afforestation of large tracts of upland Britain, has helped the kestrel by providing excellent hunting regions at the early stages of planting, and the urban environment has been comprehensively colonised. The kestrel is now a symbol of success in a bird world where publicity is often equated with rarity or pest status.

HISTORICAL GEMS

*T*he quotations which follow give an insight into how the kestrel has been perceived and treated by man over the years. A very early reference to kestrels comes in a fascinating extract from *Of Hawks and Falconry Tract V* by Thomas Brown in 1686. Using unfortunate kestrels as guinea pigs to test a cure for 'scab and blackworm' he writes:

> I have safely given six or eight grains of Mercurius Dulcis unto Kestrels and Owls, as also crude and current Quick Silver, giving the next day pellets of silver and lead.

There was no further mention of the kestrels in the text which is hardly surprising!

Killing raptors was by no means the sole prerogative of the sporting fraternity. Pursuing cultural objectives or scientific knowledge in the Victorian era often meant the demise of the subject in question. The following examples involving the kestrel would not have raised an ethical eyebrow at the time:

> . . . Selby, on the authority of an eye-witness, has recorded the fact of the Kestrel hawking cockchafers late in the evening. The observer watched the bird through a glass, and saw him dart through a swarm of insects, seize one in each claw, and eat them while flying. He returned to the charge again and again. I ascertained it beyond doubt, as I afterwards shot him. (Yarrell 1871)

Similarly, a sketch by Henry Davenport Graham in 1852 was entitled 'Shooting Kestrels in the Cathedral' and is from a portfolio by the artist entitled *The Birds of Iona: all shot upon that sacred island or in its vicinity.*

After some research, my next step was to contact local bird-watchers, gamekeepers, forest rangers, farmers and interested people to build up a picture of known breeding territories and possibly breeding details from the past 25 years. This would give me some idea of where to set up sample study plots and shed some light on the breeding performance of the kestrel. It would also enable me to enlist the help of a team of willing and capable observers to supply consistent back-up details for my own fieldwork. To this end a questionnaire was drawn up and circulated to individuals, local branches of wildlife organisations and schools.

The response was well worth the effort. Information poured in, ranging from a series of sightings in a locality to complete breeding details. One of the most bizarre replies came from an elderly gentleman in Ayr who had been a notorious egg collector in the 1940s and 1950s. He invited me to his house and produced an amazingly detailed notebook with locations of pairs and dates which he willingly allowed me to copy. From 1953 to 1961 he had removed 17 kestrel clutches (76 eggs) and, as he put it, kestrels were not even his speciality. Unfortunately, the data ended at the clutch size! He had specialised in ravens and peregrines and had also passed on the details to the Nature Conservancy Council. Revelling in the surreptitious aspect of the whole business he recounted with undisguised relish many a tale of daring exploits and close encounters with the law.

Another local worthy, Tom McCulloch from Maybole, who has spent much of his life tramping the local area, recalled climbing down the Coastal Cliff site and removing a clutch of five almost white, finely spotted eggs in the 1930s. Once more the thrill of past jaunts still generated excitement and pleasure. One lad even wrote saying that he didn't have any information on kestrels but he was a keen artist and would draw one for me. I agreed and he duly obliged. Only two people refused to help.

The net result of the second phase was details of 34 territories in the 1950s, including 21 clutch sizes from the 'oologist of ill repute' as he signed himself. One record of a clutch of ten was given by another completely reputable observer who reckoned that two hens had laid eggs in the same nest. Inevitably the clutch had been stolen.

In the 1960s there were 43 records but disappointingly only three complete breeding cycles had been noted. 1970 to 1971 was much more productive, being

Hen kestrel feeding on a meadow pipit.

fresh in people's minds, with 71 breeding pairs located and much more breeding data. In 1972 a grand total of 101 occupied territories gave the project a great start.

The exercise had been invaluable, especially in terms of the 1950s and 1960s information as it gave a good indication of how the kestrel had fared at a time when the population in many parts of Britain was under severe pressure from organochlorine pesticides (see information window on page 16).

Over the years a team of committed observers, many of whom have become great friends, have kept the information flowing and several of the study areas, which will be described shortly, were chosen not least because of the presence in the area of one of these people. It was an invigorating period and lessons were quickly learnt. Mistakes were made but gradually skills were acquired in tree climbing and abseiling as many of the nest sites required considerable physical effort to prise out their more intimate secrets. The more one works with a subject like the kestrel the more instinctive the detective work becomes.

Some of the lessons were quite painful, like the nearly fledged kestrel which stuck out a leg as I was returning it to a nest in a hawthorn tree, and pinned my lips together. It was a very lucky kestrel. Lashings of antiseptic and a tetanus injection − for me − were the order of the day and another lesson learnt in handling birds. After several initial escapades, which thankfully ended without serious mishap, I now rarely go out to do fieldwork unaccompanied.

One classic mistake was taking on just one territory too many in the day and deviating from the planned route. I found myself, in the company of my red setter suitably named Kest, in a remote corner of Ayrshire, a long way from the nearest habitation. The kestrel hen had slipped quietly off the huge stick nest, used previously by ravens, in an isolated copse of mature Scots pines. Once the decision had been made to attempt the climb it was simply a case of throwing the rope over the lowest branch − a mere eight metres up. A couple of dozen frustrating throws later and the ancient trick of tying a stone to the end of the rope finally achieved the objective. Unluckily, the rope hung well away from the trunk of the tree and necessitated a straight rope trick climb. So far so good, but the sheer effort of the final few feet and the pull over the branch used up the last of the day's allocation of adrenalin. It only took a minute to reach the rim of the massive nest but by then my legs were like jelly and the shakes had set in. Three young kestrels, dwarfed in the nest bowl, were easily ringed but they were now incidental − there was no way I could face the downward scramble. After a twenty minute wait while I tried to relax, I climbed down, ignored the negative responses from the body, swung quickly over the branch and slid gratefully to the soft moss below. I have not enjoyed climbing a Scots pine since and class them in the same mould as larch which have brittle branches and often cause the cartoon-like sight of people painfully sliding down the trunk taking all before them.

One of the main thrusts of the work was to ring young kestrels to find out what happened after they left the nest, and to this end I enrolled as a trainee ringer with the British Trust for Ornithology. I was extremely fortunate as, in the early 1970s, my trainer, the late Graham Stewart, was ringing the broods of the few remaining pairs of peregrine falcons that had survived the pesticide calamity.

I spent many evenings in the company of Dick Roxburgh, Duncan Cameron and Richard Mearns, the RSPB roving Peregrine Warden in south-west Scotland. I have vivid memories of sitting on a ledge high up on a rock holding two white falcon chicks as the adult pair hung in the air 30 metres above, the evening sun glinting on their sickle-shaped bodies – and the whoosh of the down-draught as one of the birds peeled off and dived down at terrifying speed before pulling out and rejoining its mate. I remember, too, the ferocity of older chicks which raked with their talons as we tried to sort out which legs belonged to which bird, and the sense of disappointment and futility when we came across robbed nests. Eventually I graduated to a 'C' permit which meant I could ring on my own and finally a 'Special A' permit for kestrels, which gave me full independence!

What emerged from all the preliminary ferretting was a two-phased programme of work on the kestrel. The period from 1972 to 1978 was spent collecting as much data as possible from as many territories as possible to build up an overview of the distribution, density and breeding performance of the kestrel in Ayrshire. The aim was to provide a baseline against which to check any future population changes.

Some of the information was very easy to obtain, for example distribution of the bird throughout Ayrshire. It did not take long to establish that the kestrel breeds in all forty-six 10-kilometre grid squares in Ayrshire except Lady Isle where the birds have been recorded on passage only. Ailsa Craig would have fallen into the same category but for a visit in 1980 when, on stepping off the boat, I saw a hen kestrel hunting from a fence post over the short-cropped grass round the defunct gas works. After a few minutes she gave up the position, because of the disembarking party, and flew up to join three newly fledged young on the cliffs

Dick Roxburgh and Duncan Cameron ringing young peregrines in 1974.

Ailsa Craig, 1980: the first bird I noticed was a hen kestrel hunting from a fence post.

behind the spit. None of the contacts in the county reported the species as being other than common and widespread, a subjective assessment which was borne out by our records in all the areas given special consideration. Other data such as breeding performance required years of collecting nest records to allow adequate evaluation.

Building upon a knowledge of breeding territories gained through fieldwork, and with a solid core of reliable contacts, I was able, from 1979 onwards, to closely monitor 30 sample territories each year to find out which factors were affecting the kestrels' breeding performance.

By 1990 the statistics had reached impressive levels – 400 territories known, 1,350 nest records safely on file and a total of over 1,000 kestrels ringed. I also had the field to myself in Scotland as very few people had chosen the kestrel as a subject for an in-depth study. The only exception was a friend, Andy Village, who worked on the kestrel for his Ph.D. at Edinburgh University. His study area at Eskdalemuir in the Scottish Borders is best known for its extremely high rainfall figures. Andy worked professionally on the kestrel with the Institute of Terrestrial Ecology before being called to the Church.

The importance of the Ayrshire work, albeit done on an amateur basis, lies in its timescale – a consistent level of recording for nearly 20 years. In the chapters which follow I'd like to take the reader behind the scenes in the kestrel breeding season and, through my experiences, give an insight into the lifestyle of this fascinating bird.

To protect the birds from undue disturbance and to maintain anonymity in the interests of landowners, I have given each territory mentioned in the book a fictitious name which reflects one aspect of its character.

STATUS IN BRITAIN TODAY

Estimating the current distribution of kestrels in Britain is not too difficult, estimating the density and numbers is a minefield. The position is far from uniform over the country. The intense interest generated in birds of prey following the decline attributed to pesticides led to a number of local and national surveys being carried out in the late sixties, seventies and eighties.

In 1973 the kestrel map produced by John Parslow, shows the main breeding range as being all over Britain except for the south-west tip of Ireland and eastern England where this species was described as breeding regularly but in small numbers. The other exception is Shetland where breeding ceased in 1905. In the scales adopted by Parslow it occupied the 10,001 – 100,000 pairs bracket.

A much more comprehensive picture emerged after the fieldwork for the *Atlas of Breeding Birds in Britain and Ireland* (Sharrock, 1976). Kestrels were recorded in 92 per cent of the 10-kilometre squares in Britain; Shetland was again cited as an area of absence. In the Outer Hebrides, parts of the Western Highlands and much of the Fen Country, the kestrel was recorded as being thin on the ground as a breeding bird. The terrain and its heavy rainfall may account for the lack of numbers in the Western Highlands, but in the Fen Country the scarcity can be accounted for by a combination of slow recovery from the pesticide period and loss of habitat. Sharrock concludes that the kestrel population was at, or above, the upper limit of Parslow's figures.

The most recent, and probably most accurate, statistics came from the work of the well-known raptor expert Ian Newton (1984) who reviewed the status of raptors in Britain during the previous 150 years. He writes: 'Only one species, the kestrel, can be considered as being close to the level that the available habitat could support'.

The kestrel population is rated as being stable and at approximately 70,000 breeding pairs. To put this in perspective, the nearest species in numerical terms are the sparrowhawk at 25,000 pairs and the buzzard at 12,000 pairs, while the other 12 species which breed amount to a threadbare 2,000 pairs. Although outnumbered in certain localities by the sparrowhawk and buzzard, the kestrel is still the most widespread and numerous raptor in Britain comprising a staggering 64 per cent of all breeding pairs.

THE EUROPEAN SCENE

The European kestrel has an impressive distribution, being the most abundant diurnal raptor over much of the western Palaearctic. From latitude 68–70°N, it ranges southwards over three continents, Europe, Asia and Africa. It is essentially a bird of open country, grass plains, steppes, heaths and cultivated fields, from sea level to 1500 metres.

In Europe, the bird can be resident, dispersive or partially migratory, though some individuals have been recorded in Mauritania, Libya, Ghana and Nigeria, presumably having joined the wholly migratory birds of the cooler regions on their trans-Saharan migration. The European kestrel has been recorded well out of its normal range in places like Iceland, the Faroes, Bear Island and the Azores.

There is little evidence of marked changes in the kestrel's range in Europe, but the population sizes vary considerably from country to country. In some countries it is not even the commonest raptor; for example, the lesser kestrel is more numerous than the European kestrel in Spain and Greece, and the buzzard outnumbers it in eastern Germany.

Although the published figures are far from comprehensive, the European overview at least gives some cause for optimism. Data from 25 countries is presented in Appendix 1. What emerges from the evidence is that there are 12 countries where the position can be described as stable, six where the kestrel population is increasing after a decline and nine where decline is still continuing.

Massive problems still exist, not least the continued use of pesticides and the senseless slaughter of raptors in the name of sport in countries such as Italy, France and Germany. The birds are particulary vulnerable at strategic points on migratory routes, such as Malta where the carnage is horrendous. An estimated 500 – 1,000 kestrels are shot annually on Malta, only one or two pairs breed and not even on an annual basis.

This is despite partial or total protective legislation being on the statute books of most countries. The implementation of the law is often incredibly difficult where traditional practices, a strong lobby from the hunting fraternities, not to mention sheer prejudice and ignorance, must be overcome. Britain stands well clear at the top of the kestrel league table in Europe; Spain, with approximately 30,000 pairs, comes next. Britain also holds very significant breeding stocks of other European raptors like the golden eagle, hen harrier and peregrine falcon.

THE WORLD SCENE

The kestrel is one of 287 species which make up the order Falconiformes and belongs to the family Falconidae (caracaras, falcons and falconets). The European kestrel, *Falco tinnunculus* is one of ten species of typical kestrels in the genus *Falco* (35 species) which also contains the spectacular peregrine and gyrfalcon. They are mostly medium-sized falcons, characterised by long, pointed wings, short but powerful bills which have a distinct notch on each side, short legs and strong feet. The female is usually larger than the male which, in turn, is more colourful.

The range and status of the different kestrels could not be more polarised. One species, the American kestrel, is found in both North and South America, from Alaksa and Canada to Tierra del Fuego. Its extensive geographic range is matched by its capacity to survive in virtually all major terrestrial habitats below the tree line in the

New World. Even the Atlantic Ocean has not proved to be an insurmountable barrier to this small falcon, as a male American kestrel was seen on Fair Isle, Shetland in May 1976. The Australian or nankeen kestrel also has a wide distribution in Australia and New Guinea, and the lesser kestrel breeds in Mediterranean countries but ranges as far east as China.

Some kestrels are very limited in their ranges and are confined to islands. The Seychelles, Madagascar, East Indies and Mauritius all have their endemic species. Limited to an area of gorges and mountains to the south-west of the island, the Mauritius kestrel has the dubious status of being one of the rarest birds in the world. Severe reduction of numbers and distribution of the bird has resulted from a combination of massive habitat loss and competition from introduced species. Captive breeding programmes have so far succeeded in supplementing the remaining breeding pairs in the wild, and the release of young birds has given the population a real chance of staving off extinction.

The kestrel species are listed below:

European kestrel	*Falco tinnunculus*	Eurasia, Africa & India
Moluccan kestrel	*F. moluccensis*	East Indies
Australian kestrel	*F. cenchroides*	Australia & New Guinea
Madagascar kestrel	*F. newtoni*	Madagascar & Aldabra
Mauritius kestrel	*F. punctatus*	Mauritius
Seychelles kestrel	*F. araea*	Seychelles
American kestrel	*F. sparverius*	New World
Lesser kestrel	*F. naumanni*	Mediterranean
Greater or white-eyed kestrel	*F. rupicoloides*	Kenya, Tanzania, South Africa & Somalia
Fox kestrel	*F. alopex*	Ghana to Sudan, South Ethiopia & Kenya

In addition, there are four other species which are regarded as aberrant kestrels.

Red-footed kestrel	*F. vespertinus*	Central Europe & Asia
Grey kestrel	*F. ardosiaceus*	Savannal regions of Africa
Dickinson's kestrel	*F. dickinsoni*	Tanzania south to Portuguese East Africa & west to Angola
Madagascar banded kestrel	*F. zoniventris*	Madagascar

There are several endemic races of *Falco tinnunculus*, for example, *alexandri* and *neglectus* (Cape Verde Islands), *canariensis* and *dacotiae* (Canary Islands) and the Arabian and Egyptian race *rupicolaeformis*, which is largely resident but has been known to visit the Sudan.

WINTER INTO SPRING

*E*ven in February, when winter can still have a vicious sting in its tail, preparatory work is well in hand for the season ahead. A new year-file is open and already holds licences for disturbing birds like the merlin, peregrine falcon and barn owl which are encountered in the fieldwork. Permission to catch and ring 25 adult kestrels has been applied for and granted by the Nature Conservancy Council. Landowners, like the Forestry Commission, have been contacted to ensure access to the study areas, and licences have been renewed by the British Trust for Ornithology to cover the ringing operations. A supply of rings has been bought, the traps overhauled and all the gear checked. This inevitable, but necessary, paperwork is part of the overall control of fieldwork exercised by the Government and non-statutory organisations to ensure minimum disruption to the wildlife species which are being studied.

At a local level the co-ordination of work on birds of prey in south-west Scotland is done by the Raptor Study Group. There are six such groups covering the major regions in Scotland linked by the RSPB, Investigation Section. Informal meetings of enthusiastic fieldworkers are held twice a year, once in early spring to determine the strategy for the season ahead, and again in September to analyse the results. Our group meets at Culzean and cars converge from as far away as Glasgow, Dumfries and Stranraer. In February current issues are discussed, priorities assessed, problems aired, ways of preventing duplication worked out and Rosie's baking consumed! Such is the nature of the work that we see each other infrequently in the next five months, but the telephones are often red hot. From now onwards there are several raptor widows.

The over-riding feeling is one of keen anticipation tempered with uncertainty as the permutations of natural and man-made factors which will determine the eventual outcome of the season for birds like the kestrel are, as yet, unknown. What is certain is that the weather and fitness will play a big hand in the lives of both kestrels and fieldworkers. The moments of success will doubtless be preceded by many fruitless, frustrating hours of searching and waiting. No two seasons are ever the same.

One task, which acts as an appetiser, is checking the nest boxes in two of the upland areas. Traditionally the first outing is to the Carrick Forest preceded by a call to Robin Heaney, the Senior Ranger, to confirm that there are no conflicts with forestry operations. Robin has his finger firmly on the pulse of what is happening in his district and a chat can often save miles of leg work. Usually, the forest is deceptively empty as I drive over the rough roads through ranks of solid sitka, but a red or roe deer is normally seen up one of the rides or crossing the track. Both species have made full use of this artificial man-made environment to the point where numbers are extremely high and, due to the dense cover, control by the ranger staff is difficult.

Surprisingly, a tawny owl is regularly seen on these drives, perched by the roadside or hunting the verge. Several pairs eke out an existence in the forest and one territory has a fascinating pedigree. All three nests found recently have been on the ground in the vicinity of Robin's house. One year the birds nested among the grass and rushes under one of the road bridges, in a very open situation, rearing one young. Next year a brood of three was reared under Robin's wood shed. 1986 surpassed everything as the birds nested on the gravel in the narrow recess between a large flower pot and the wall of the house. The sitting bird tended to face the wall and was rarely bothered by human activity. A classic case of 'if I can't see them, they can't see me'! Unfortunately the sharp stones were not ideal nest liners and all three eggs eventually cracked and the bird deserted.

The journey ends where the tree cover meets the open hillside. Nest boxes had been erected along the forest edge a few years before when the adjoining sheep pasture had been bought and planted by the Forestry Commission; my aim being to check the kestrels' response to new hunting grounds which had an ample supply of nest sites. Work in Holland in the 1960s had shown that kestrels readily

A long-eared owl aggressively displaying at the camera lens.

took to this type of simulated nest hole, the boxes having been erected on tall poles in open ground.

My boxes were placed in the semi-mature sitka but, despite kestrels hunting the area extensively and using them as winter roosts, to date they have shown a marked reluctance to use them for nesting. The boxes are the standard, open-fronted structures recommended in all the literature and I would never be forgiven if I didn't mention Jim Murdoch, Culzean's former minibus driver, who constructed many of them.

Hopes had soared one year when a pair of kestrels had been seen regularly in the vicinity of one nest box in early spring, but the eventual tenants were a pair of long-eared owls. They laid a clutch of five eggs, deserted for some reason, then relaid in the next nest box along the line. This time they completed the cycle. The opportunity was taken to set up a hide for photography and one of my most abiding memories is of the brooding adult aggressively displaying at the camera

*L*ONG-EARED OWL

Probably one of our most secretive and under-recorded birds, the long-eared owl is found in very similar habitat to the kestrel in Ayrshire, often sharing small shelter belts in upland areas for breeding. A pair of long-eared owls nested only 20 metres from the kestrel nest box at Waterhead and, at the Magpie Wood territory nearby, a crow's nest was first used by the owls then the kestrels in successive years. The long-eared owl does not normally use the same nest site in consecutive years.

At close range the deep orange eyes of the long-eared owl are its most striking feature, eclipsing the usually conspicuous 'ear tufts'. These tufts have nothing to do with hearing and have a recognition, signalling function. During the daytime, the bird prefers to roost in thick cover, usually next to the trunk of a tree, and is difficult to locate.

The long-eared owl is an early nester, clutches being laid between late March and early April, usually in the disused nests of crows, herons, magpies or even squirrels. There are records of clutches in February. The female is very sensitive to disturbance at egg laying and early incubation and may desert. Second clutches are often laid if the first is lost and there are records of second broods but these are rare. Broods of three are normal and as the chicks near fledging their defensive display is impressive. The feathers are puffed up and the wings raised as they endeavour to portray a much bigger and fiercer creature than they actually are.

Although the British population is sedentary there are irregular invasions of continental and Scandinavian birds, the winter of 1975/76 being particularly well documented. In Finland, 80 per cent of long-eared owls are nomadic and breed only when their prey is abundant. The British population is widespread but irregularly spaced. There has been a decline since 1900 which coincides with the increase in the tawny owl population. The tawny owl has similar needs and competes effectively against the long-eared owl. Recent estimates put the latest population at over 3,000 breeding pairs but unlikely to exceed 10,000.

NEST BOXES FOR KESTRELS

Kestrels take readily to nest boxes especially in areas where natural sites are lacking and prey is abundant. This was dramatically illustrated in the late 1950s and early 1960s in both Switzerland and Holland. In the Swiss example 36 boxes were erected near Basle in an area of featureless polder, approximately 2,000 hectares in size. No less than 26 were occupied by kestrels.

The work in the Dutch polders achieved the same direct response from kestrels when rows of boxes were erected in the open on two-metre poles. In Scotland, boxes erected in commercial forestry ground at Eskdalemuir were colonised as were those in two of the Ayrshire study areas. However, the mere erecting of nest boxes does not guarantee occupation, as was witnessed in at least three Forestry Commission areas.

The standard kestrel nest box is a large, open-fronted box with an overhanging roof. Measurements are noted in Figure 1. Either a half front or slightly less gives added protection, though kestrels have used nest boxes with entrance holes as small as ten centimetres square. I prefer to give the birds room for easy access and also give the young the opportunity to survey their local area before fledging.

Sandy gravel or ground peat have been used for the base material but I usually insert the central core of a disused carrion crow's nest to give the box a more natural interior. The main need is for a substrate soft enough for the kestrel to scrape a depression for the clutch.

The box should be situated in a site which gives the birds an easy flight line in and, if possible, difficulty of access to casual human observers. In order to ensure a greater chance of occupancy, the box should be erected well in advance of March when nest prospecting begins. Be prepared for opportunist lodgers such as jackdaws, long-eared owls and even doves.

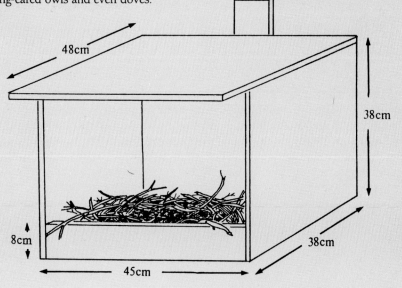

Figure 1
Open-fronted nest box.

*Renewing nest boxes
in the Carrick Forest
in January.*

lens, the next box almost obliterated by the show of feather power as it puffed itself up to double its normal size. Wings outstretched and orange eyes gleaming – it was a fearsome sight.

The whole character of the forest has changed since the 1970s when I first became involved in the area. At that time fifteen pairs of kestrels nested in or around the newly planted forest using the many cliff faces or mature Scots pine trees as nest sites. Putting aside the controversy surrounding blanket sitka spruce monoculture forestry, there is little doubt that the first stages of forest development are a productive and dynamic environment for the kestrel. Now only two or three pairs grace the fringes as the suffocating tree cover has markedly reduced the hunting ranges. I will continue to visit the study area but now content myself with the supporting cast of blackcock, curlew, the moth-like short-eared owl and the foraging fox.

The second upland area, which I'll call Waterhead, is characterised by small isolated stands of spruce scattered over very open sheep pasture. Slowly the ranks of sitka are encroaching on all sides but the area, measuring four kilometres by three, still holds a viable population of kestrels which do use my nest boxes. The contrast between both these upland habitats and lowland coastal Culzean in February and early March is total. In the Culzean Country Park, tawny owls, mute swans and herons are on eggs and the signs of spring are evident with the emerging ground flora of dog's mercury and daffodils. In the hills, the ground is bare and brown, the birdlife is sparse and conditions can usually be described as 'character building'. It's little wonder that kestrels prefer to winter on the coastal hinterland.

Each of the six small woods has supported breeding pairs of kestrels in the last ten years, all but one in nest boxes. My strategy here was to erect the nest boxes on the exact site which had been used by the kestrel in the previous season. Instead of discarding the old crow's platform, it was inserted in the bottom of the box to act as a natural base. The ploy certainly worked.

Mike Callan, one of the Park's ranger team, normally accompanied me on these rigorous early season forays and we took it in turns to climb the trees and check the condition of the boxes. Neither of us relished the task, especially if a box needed to be replaced or relocated, but it's a great way of breaking in for the season. I've estimated that in one season I climb the equivalent in height of a return trip up Goat Fell on Arran (874 metres) and Mike must do more in his quest for nests to photograph. Mike is a fanatical wildlife photographer and puts in an incredible number of hours in the field – the prerogative of a single man!

If a box has to be moved both of us need to be up the tree at the same time, and only those who have wrestled with these delightful sitka spruce can appreciate the amount of fine dust and debris which is disturbed even on a straightforward climb. If the tree has been climbed a few times the resin can be another hazard as it weeps from the debarked footholds. When manoeuvring a box at a height of ten metres the penetrating needles always seem to find inroads into unprotected flesh. The redeeming features of these much-maligned trees are the number of branches on each tree and their relative strength. I feel quite safe at heights of fifteen to twenty metres.

Sometimes there is a surprise in store, even on the most severe of days. An early March visit to Waterhead in 1987 was nearly abandoned due to the depth of the snow which had fallen on the hills. Access to the area had been by courtesy of a snow plough and we waded through thigh-deep drifts to the wood. Inside the plantation the ground was churned up, evidence of it having served as a haven for sheep during the storm.

Waterhead: standard design of kestrel nest box.

The nest box was still in position but a check was necessary to see if it was still stable. My first sitka spruce of the year and it didn't feel too bad despite the blown snow adhering to the trunk. The box was fine, the scrape untouched as expected, but a couple of pellets on the rim looked reasonably fresh. I almost missed the kestrel. It was the flapping of a loose wing which caught the eye. The bird, a hen, was lying crumpled on one of the outer branches just below the box. She was frozen stiff and closer inspection on the ground revealed that she was not a casualty of last season, but had died within the last fortnight. She weighed in at a paltry 135 g and the breast bone was devoid of muscle. She was also unringed. There were no signs of a violent death and one can only assume that the open spell had attracted her back to the breeding territory prematurely but her poor condition and the severity of the last cold snap had caused her to succumb. What a start.

Figure 2
Waterhead study area.
All the territory names
are fictitious though the
locations are accurate.

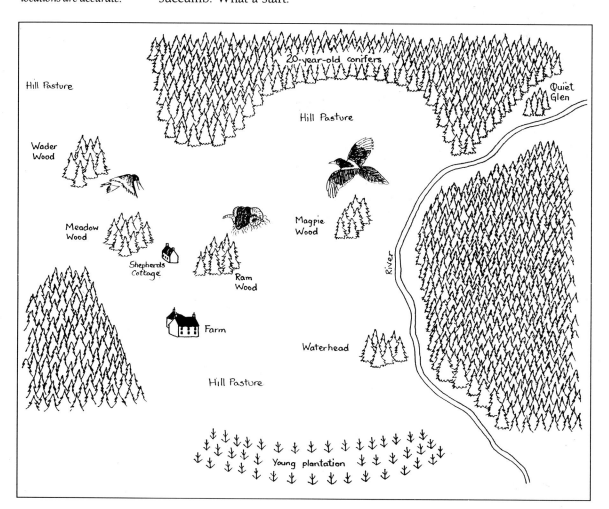

Every year a minimum of six visits are made to each of the selected territories in order to record information on the main stages of the breeding season. The data required is: whether the territory is occupied, the date on which the first eggs are laid, the final clutch size (adults are caught and ringed at this stage), the hatching data, the brood size (when the young are ringed) and the fledging success or otherwise. In reality, it can take more than a dozen visits to complete the picture for each territory.

Time-consuming and very technical methods of research like radio telemetry, when birds are tracked using transmitters, or genetic fingerprinting, are usually outside the scope of the amateur ornithologist. However, their role in monitoring consistently over a long period of time with accurate fieldwork provides extremely valuable back up for the professionals in assessing national populations and trends.

Mike Callan with a winter casualty at Waterhead.

AFFORESTATION AND THE KESTREL

The recovery of the kestrel and other birds of prey from the pesticide-induced lows of the 1950s corresponded with a major change in land use which for once worked in favour of certain raptors, such as the kestrel, short-eared owl and hen harrier, especially in upland Scotland.

Afforestation on a grand scale by both the Forestry Commission and private enterprises began in earnest in the mid 1960s and peaked in the mid 1970s. Thousands of hectares of upland moorland and sheep run were fenced, fertilised and planted with monoculture conifers, sitka spruce in the main, radically altering the landscape and, in the short term, providing ideal conditions for certain raptor prey species.

The exclusion of sheep and the upgrading of ground by regular applications of fertiliser encouraged a healthy grass regime which, in turn, provided ideal habitat for short-tailed field voles which naturally attracted breeding kestrels.

Provided that nest sites were readily available the density of kestrels in these newly planted forests was very high, pairs often tolerating very close neighbours as happened in a newly planted area in Dumfriesshire where vole numbers peaked in 1975. Two adjacent glens supported 10 pairs, 6 pairs nesting along one long stretch of rock face rearing 23 young.

However, when the forest canopy begins to close after six or seven years, suppressing the ground vegetation, the voles are much less common and the kestrel population dwindles. Eventually when the forest becomes more mature and more suitable for sparrowhawks, the kestrels tend to be found on the fringes only where there is easy access to open ground.

Although the scale of planting has decreased or levelled off in many forests, the second generation plantings are coming on-stream and it will be interesting to see how the kestrels respond. The ground will certainly not be burned and cleared to enable the lush grassland to reappear and this new habitat of thicker undergrowth may not be ideal for a hunter of small mammals due to the cover afforded to the prey. The small bird populations will, however, be much stronger.

A lot will depend upon the landscaping of modern forests. Techniques such as retaining open glades for deer management, planting well back from stream and river beds and leaving poorer ground unplanted will ensure that there is a place for the kestrel even in the higher age classes of forestry.

ON SITE SEARCH

Great efforts are made in late March and April to record whether or not a territory is occupied by kestrels, as the accuracy of the monitoring depends upon following each breeding attempt through from beginning to end. This is absolutely fundamental as a territory can be occupied early in the season and the attempt may fail even before an egg is laid. If these failures are not detected then there will be a bias in the results towards successful pairs, thus distorting the final picture for the season.

For me it is one of the most exciting parts of the season as years of experience and skill as a fieldworker are put to the acid test. It's difficult to put into words the feelings which you have on arriving in a territory, to be met by the sight of a hen kestrel perched on the top of a sitka spruce tree close to the traditional nest site. It's like a reunion with an old friend.

The task of locating the pairs is made easier by the fact that the birds are more obvious in these early months, both visually and vocally, than at any time in the cycle other than when the young are fledging. Even so, the first visits must be tempered with extreme caution as very often you only get one chance, a glimpse of a bird or maybe a quiet call from the middle of the wood. It is worth taking at least a quarter of an hour, or longer, to survey the scene from a distance with binoculars before moving in to search. The car can be a useful hide if the road is conveniently placed. Strathclyde Regional Council has thoughtfully designed at least five lay-bys in Ayrshire with kestrel viewing in mind! On one memorable occasion a kestrel hen flew from the nest and proceeded to have a dust bath in a sheep rub within easy binocular distance of the car. At all times you must be prepared to match the kestrel's capacity for sitting motionless for hours on end.

The ability to distinguish the kestrel from other birds of prey and to differentiate between the sexes is obviously vital in fieldwork of this kind. A full description of the bird is given on page 36; it is enough here to point out the main field markings which aid quick identification. The kestrel's bold behaviour, strong markings and hovering technique of hunting, allied to its angular shape are important in setting it apart from the sparrowhawk with which it is most often

SPOT THE KESTREL

The kestrel is not large, having a body length of 32–35 cm. In relation to the body, the wings and tail seem long and give an angular, sharp outline to the bird. The wings when closed are about 2 cm shorter than the tail. The head is large and flattened on top, and the shoulders are broad as is the case with most falcons. There is a great deal of strength packed into its small compact frame belying its lightness. Basically, the kestrel is an extremely efficient killing machine and is as tenacious as any other raptor.

Though there is the normal dissimilarity in size between the sexes, it is not as pronounced as in the peregrine or merlin. The cock bird is slightly smaller (136–252 g) than the hen (154–314 g). Male and female kestrels share several features in common. The eyes are large, with a dark brown iris, and the short, powerful bill, with the typical falcon notch, is blue-grey at the tip – shading to grey at the base. The cere, the orbital ring and the legs are chrome yellow and the claws are black. The legs are short and powerful to withstand the considerable impact of taking prey on the ground, unlike the long precision instruments of the sparrowhawk which takes prey in flight. Kestrels have an acute sense of hearing, are on the alert most of the time and are normally silent away from the nest site.

Seen at close quarters, the cock kestrel is a most attractive bird and its plumage pattern is striking both when at rest or in flight. The crown and nape are a distinctive ash grey, contrasting strongly with the rich, chestnut, black-spotted back. The black spots are drop-shaped and vary in size and number. The flight feathers are a darker brown-black colour, while the 13–15 cm grey-blue tail sports a broad, black, sub-terminal band and narrow white tip. Feathers on the thighs give a 'baggy pants' look similar to the rook. The black facial moustache is more prominent than the hen's, and older cock birds tend to have bolder patterns.

By comparison, the hen is a more uniform chestnut above providing excellent camouflage when on the nest. The upper back and mantle is also chestnut, but is heavily barred with black. The rump and upper tail coverts are blue-grey. Along the length of the tail are closely packed, blackish-brown bars and, apart from the black, sub-terminal band, the ground colour is pale chestnut sometimes tinged with grey. The amount of grey can vary enormously from hen to hen.

The juvenile bird does pose problems in identification as it is very similar to the adult female in plumage. Juveniles are usually paler in colour, including the yellow cere and legs, but there is considerable variation in colour especially in relation to the grey on the tail. Full adult plumage is acquired at the age of two and a half to three years, moults taking place gradually. The first moult is between August and the following April, another during the second spring, then the sequence is completed in the third moult by the third summer.

PATTERNS OF TERRITORY OCCUPATION

Territories can be occupied throughout the year, especially in lowland habitats but on the whole kestrels tend to be non-territorial in behaviour during winter. There are several patterns of territory occupation which occur but these vary from district to district, year to year, as kestrels respond to differences in environmental conditions such as food availability and competition for nest sites.

In any district there are basically two types of nesting territories. The traditional territories are occupied usually on an annual basis and the secondary territories occupied only when the population is high and food is abundant. The planting of upland hill pasture for forestry purposes can often stimulate an increase in population due to the increased food availability and for the first six or seven years after planting the kestrels use primary and secondary territories to utilise the favourable conditions. When the canopy closes and food supplies diminish the kestrel population invariably falls, the secondary territories are vacated and the kestrels revert to the old pattern of traditional territories.

A second pattern which occurs occasionally in upland areas is clumping. This arises in areas where the only nest sites are in a glen or valley and the surrounding area are excellent for hunting. Close nesting of birds will occur with birds tolerating near neighbours. One early record relates:

> At Craig Lough on the line of the Roman wall, a few miles east of Haltwhistle, I have seen nests within 10 yards and in one case 7 nests in a linear distance of 40 yards.

> In some lowland farming areas where the environment is stable, the pattern is very uniform with nesting territories spaced quite uniformly. Six territories were spread evenly along one 20 kilometre stretch of the Ayrshire coastline.

confused. The sparrowhawk has a more rounded wing outline. In the kestrel the sexes are dissimilar. The attractively coloured cock bird is in complete contrast to the more uniform chestnut hen. Concentrate on features like the head and tail which are quite diagnostic even at a distance. The cock bird has a distinctive ash-grey crown and nape and a very grey-blue tail with a strong sub terminal band and white tip which are most obvious when the bird is hovering and the tail fanned. All along the length of the hen's tail are closely packed blackish brown bars which are also very clear when the bird is hovering. The back of the hen is also barred and the head brown while the cock bird's back is a rich chestnut colour spotted with black. Compared to working with some birds of prey species it does not take long to become competent at sorting out the kestrel.

Similarly an understanding of the pre-laying behaviour of the kestrel is vital if the birds' activities are to be interpreted correctly. The bond between a breeding pair, which is sustained long after the breeding season is over, often has a turbulent start as kestrels select and compete for mates and nesting territories. Migrant kestrels settle on prospective territories from late February onwards, though some lowland sites can sustain one or even a pair of birds throughout the winter. The cock bird seems to have a greater attachment to a nesting territory in winter. Kestrels are quick to take up suitable territories when they fall vacant. One barn owl territory occupied for ten years in succession fell vacant when the owls disappeared after severe weather in February. Kestrels had moved in within a fortnight.

Much of the early season action is related to territorial defence, courtship display and nest site selection. Naturally, seeing a kestrel mobbing ravens, carrion crows or even another kestrel above a nesting territory is a good indicator. In response to the arrival of a competitor in the territory, the incumbent cock bird will fly directly at the intruder and if this fails the birds will engage in aerial combat. Chasing and buffeting the opponent using wings and talons, are both employed to discourage the interloper. These encounters can be prolonged and injury can be sustained. The ferocity and intensity of the encounter can make enthralling viewing. Cock kestrels will also fight over a hen and hen kestrels will likewise vie for the attentions of a cock bird as I witnessed at Culzean one year. I was viewing one of the Park's kestrel territories from a rock promontory when, alerted by the noise, I spotted two birds skirmishing in mid-air above the cliffline.

The birds, both hens, were in full chase, flying rapidly through the trees calling and chattering, then soaring up and occasionally baring talons in mid-air. A cock bird was eventually spotted sitting in a tree, taking quite a bit of notice of the proceedings and being chaperoned by a pair of carrion crows. After a few minutes, the kestrel which seemed to have the upper hand landed on the nesting ledge on the cliff, gave it a cursory inspection, then flew up and resumed the struggle. The intensity of the encounter increased until finally both birds fluttered down to land on a grassy bank just above high tide mark. Still locked together by their grappling talons they fought it out. Both birds were on their backs, supported by their outstretched wings, lashing viciously at each other. The crows, ever keen to take advantage of a situation, flew down to investigate and in the process galvanised the cock bird into action. He stooped down from his vantage point to mount an attack on the crows. Unfortunately the intervention disturbed the hen kestrels and their engagement was deferred. All three kestrels joined forces to harass the crows which lost no time in departing. The kestrels settled down on perches in the trees and although no further action was observed it was obvious that the less dominant hen was well away from the other birds.

The conflict can be fatal and occasionally birds have been found near nest sites in spring with severe head wounds. Although kestrels are monogamous there are several examples of polygamous behaviour. In complete contrast to the situation described above, I have seen two hens attending the same nest site near the end of the incubation period, showing no aggression towards each other with only one cock bird in the vicinity. Unfortunately children robbed the site and observations ceased.

In a one-to-one situation courtship involves aerial display, food passing and joint nest site inspection. The aerial displays can involve both birds at one time or just the cock bird with the hen perched near or at the prospective nest site. Soaring above the nest site, soaring together, diving at one another and chasing are all components of displaying. The cock bird often circles above the hen and dives in short stoops, swinging up vertically after each stoop and occasionally coming very close to physical contact. One pair were seen to grapple in mid-air and had a near catastrophic end as they dropped like stones only pulling apart a few metres above the hillside. They were either very good or very lucky.

The culmination of the activity is often copulation or nest inspection. Copulation often occurs more than two months before egg laying and is initiated by the hen which adopts an invitation posture. The cock bird responds by approaching and mounting the hen, maintaining its balance by way of rapid wing beats and spread tail. Mating lasts for 10–45 seconds and takes place regularly during the weeks prior to egg laying. The hen's most fertile period is just before laying when she is forming eggs. I have recorded copulation well after the full clutch has been laid. Both sexes have been recorded choosing the nest site and when the birds fly in they have a special flight pattern with the wings held high above the body.

One of the most fascinating aspects of the kestrel breeding cycle is the division of labour between the sexes. There is some overlap of roles but in the main the cock bird assumes the role of provider thus complementing the hen's role as the nest site manageress. It is therefore more likely on the early visits to spot a hen hanging round the general area of the nest site.

There is no doubt that one of the many appeals in working with kestrels is that they nest in very interesting places which often pose a challenge to the intrepid amateur. Many of the territories have been traditionally occupied by kestrels for decades but even so the task of locating the birds can be far from straightforward. One of the problems is that my kestrel passion is pursued outside my normal work as Principal and Chief Ranger at Culzean Country Park. A spell of blank evenings in early spring, when no progress is made, can result in a backlog of sites to visit and general frustration. A look at some of the territories most consistently used by kestrels will give some idea of the kestrel's requirements and illustrate some of the problems encountered and techniques employed to pin down the pairs.

Two of the most predictable territories are the Dams. Both territories are remarkably similar in habitat mixture, are situated less than a kilometre apart and are under the protective custody of Scottish Power. Over the last 15 years, successive pairs of kestrels have nested in the inspection chambers in the central towers which dominate the dam structures. The surrounding area is a mix of mature deciduous woodland, fringe upland grassland harbouring voles, scrub woodland rich in small bird populations and lowland pasture. There has been

Successive kestrel pairs have nested at the Dam over the past two decades.

virtually no change in the composition of either territory recently.

Access depends upon timing. Successive engineers based at the Dams have taken a special interest in the birds' welfare and phone in with arrival dates and other vital information. If the contacts are around when we arrive, the gates are opened and it's a leisurely walk along the walkway to the tower. Oystercatchers herald your passage as the ledges are scanned for signs of recently plucked prey or fresh droppings. Sheltered roosting and preening perches are usually found within easy reach of the nest site. The door is opened quietly just in case a kestrel is in. Three steps and you're above the heavy trap door and are able to peer through the small hole designed to hold the lifting bar. Most of the chamber below can be checked, even the nest site at the foot of the ladder, and if the bird is in residence you can observe then leave without disturbing the scene − always a bonus.

However, if the gates are closed, then it's down the wooded slopes to the river below and a scramble over boulders to the base of the metal ladder. One hazard is the cascade from the dam overflow which can be prohibitive even for the adventurous. There is the possibility of a roosting barn owl in the valve housing or a heron fishing in one of the ponds or even a flash of otter. All that is left now is to climb the 20 metres up the ladder.

Pellets which have accumulated at the base of the ladder can be an early clue. The last few rungs are taken slowly as a departing kestrel can be unnerving at that height. A few breast feathers discarded during preening, a pellet or tufts of fur from a plucked vole are always welcome indicators. The grey mass of pellet and nest debris which has built up over the years behind the ladder will be scraped to form a bowl for the eggs if the birds are established. As in most territories there are alternative sites which may be used. In the case of the Dams there are a number of ledge sites in the adjacent quarries which provided some of the building material for the water barriers. Not once since the work began has the journey to the Dams been fruitless, at least one of the two being occupied annually.

The Limekilns is, by contrast, virtually treeless and is situated in the midst of a wide expanse of upland sheep pasture. Again, kestrels have nested there for decades and in one exceptional year, when voles were superabundant, three pairs reared young. It is a brooding, eerie place, reached only by a 20 minute walk from the nearest parking place. In spring, bubbling curlew and rising skylarks fill the air and plump wheatears, white rumps flashing, skip along the dyke tops just out of camera range. The villains of the piece are the greater black-backed gulls which join the carrion crows to scour the hillside for helpless lambing ewes and casualties. Wallace, the farmer, is usually heard before he is seen, whistling the dogs into action or roaring up the tracks on his scrambler. He can generally say if the birds are in residence. Lambing is a very sensitive time and great care must be taken to liaise with the farmers and cause minimum disturbance while crossing their land.

First port of call is the old kilns which stand by the burn. Two holes near the top of the front walls are the most likely spots and the grassy tussocks at the entrance are checked. If the birds have been prospecting, then the grass is often flattened. Whether signs are found or not, I cannot resist a walk up to the caverns which were hewn out to supply the ore. You walk up the gully formed by the spoil heaps on one side, long since grassed over, and the exposed cliffline. On the other

Deirdre Mackinnon running the gauntlet of the Dam overflow.

side huge, gaping holes disappear into blackness 20 metres below. The flooded chambers have claimed many careless sheep over the years. The ledges above the cavern entrances are ideal for the kestrels and six have been used in my time. All require rope work to check and with the drop below it is not the safest of locations.

Ravens have recently returned to breed after an absence of 15 years which is extremely encouraging as numbers of pairs have decreased markedly in the south-west of Scotland as sheep pasture has been swallowed up by forestry interests. Lack of carrion on the ground has obviously been an important factor in the decline. The huge bulky nest on the cliff will no doubt be utilised by many kestrels in the future. Four young were reared in the nest in 1989. One absentee is the barn owl pair which formerly nested in a hole in the banking. Thankfully they have not left the area, merely moved location to a nearby farm. If the wind is favourable and great care is taken, then the resident foxes may be seen. A huge rockfall in the past resulted in a boulder field, tailor made for this successful rogue. The cubs use the grassy bankings as playgrounds, rolling stones down or playfully tumbling. It is a very special place.

Many of these traditional sites are very stable and nothing had prepared me for the traumatic change in the Gable End site in 1987. This territory was a mix of heather moor and rough pasture, the kestrel alternating between a hole in the gable end of an old steading building, a ledge in a small quarry or a selection of ledges in a superb rocky gully ten minutes' walk over the hill. If the gates are locked then it's a half-hour walk in, but short-eared owls lazily flapping over the ditches like huge moths, or hen harriers quartering the ground, are on the menu.

There is also the company of Duncan Cameron, who has helped with

The Limekilns nest site in the midst of upland sheep pasture.

Duncan Cameron views the transformed sheep pasture at the Gable End.

information since the very early days. His turn of phrase, quick-fire repartee and tales of bygone exploits make the time pass quickly. Apart from climbing either cliff or trees which are now anathema to him after numerous painful experiences, his worst fear is to meet another mallard hen coming out of a hole in ivy which should have contained a kestrel. The terrified mallard scored a direct hit with a monumental spread of droppings as it exploded into flight over his ginger scalp! Luckily there was a stream nearby for ablutions.

Afforestation on a grand scale has now completely transformed the hillside into a vivid pattern of drains and furrows. The roadway which ran to the farm has now been extended into the new forest and the Gable End nest hole is now level with the road at a distance of less than 10 metres. Undeterred, the kestrel has persevered and still sits on eggs despite the volume of traffic and new vulnerability of the site.

The heavily vegetated cliffs at Kenbain.

Very little open grassland space has been designed in this new forest but the kestrel will probably continue to breed even after the trees have grown up as the rocky gully is next to heather moor which as yet has not been converted to sitka. As it already holds a pair of hen harriers and merlins it could become very crowded for raptors; who'd be a dipper in that burn? The kestrel has used the rock ledges in the past while the merlins and hen harriers nest on the ground in the heather bankings. Unfortunately persecution by the gamekeeper is intense and neither of the latter two species has had much success. The merlin nested in an old crow's nest in a small birch tree one year but the young disappeared after 10 days. Both these species are in need of special protective measures today as their numbers are depressed far below what Scotland could support.

No matter how well you know an area it's amazing how difficult it can be to home in on the nest site. One classic example was the Kenbain territory in 1986. There are a minimum of eight nest sites which have been used in the last 15 years spread along a kilometre of rocky coastline backed by ivy-covered cliffs. Ailsa Craig provides the backdrop, fulmars float along the cliff top or wheel out to sea in great circles, gannets plunge into the sea offshore and black guillemots sneak into caves to nest. This piece of coastline has a long history of cave dwelling, spiced by the legend of Sawny Bean and his tribe of robbers and cannibals.

In the reign of James I, this terrible family sustained themselves by robbing and killing unsuspecting travellers who used the coastal route to Stranraer. Their base was in a cave at a rocky promontory only accessible at extreme low tide. His eventual capture and demise on the gallows is an integral part of S. R. Crockett's local adventure story *The Grey Man*.

The first visit to the Kenbain site had been fruitless, not a kestrel in sight, and only a carrion crow on five eggs in the ivy to show for a couple of hours' foraging. The next evening was slightly more positive as the cock bird was spotted on an old ivy branch in the middle of one of the cliff faces. The light was fading fast and he was in the middle of an elaborate preening session. Once the breast feathers had been well and truly reshuffled, he turned his attentions to the area under his wings, finally spreading his faultless tail. Every now and again he paused, settled down on the perch and ruffled the plumage until, finally, he hunched down on the perch all his feathers puffed out. At one point he called plaintively, perhaps to a hen sitting close by in a hole, but no reply was forthcoming. After half an hour, making sure his feathers were just right, he gave a last call and flew up to a ledge and, head under wing, settled down for the night.

Undaunted, yet another spell was spent at the cliff later in the week. After all the sites had been thoroughly checked to no avail it was back to the vigil in the car. Two hours later, the hen flew in and landed on a ledge, followed immediately by the cock bird. She disappeared while he took up station at the entrance. Success at last. We drove off confident that a visit next week would show eggs in the nest.

Diary extract — 27 May:

A break in the evening, a small sunny time-capsule between vicious fronts of driving rain, so a dash down the coast to check out the Kenbain pair. Fulmars were really enjoying the gusting 80 kilometre per hour wind, toying contemptuously with the updraughts. The cock kestrel left the cliff as the car pulled up, but not far from the site identified last week. We clambered up the cliff and I roped up as a precaution but it was not the climbing, but the jungle of burnet rose and bramble which caused the problems. Adding insult to injury was the sight of a fulmar incubating a fresh-laid egg in the 'certain' kestrel ledge. Back to the drawing board.

Luckily the rock face can be comfortably viewed from the car and we settled back to wait. The crow came in, tentatively at first, hopping along the fence posts, then, in like a rocket to cover the four eggs and a newly hatched chick. The break finally came after an hour. The cock bird came in with a young decapitated meadow pipit. He was in full view, perched on his length of ivy, feathers rippling in the wind. The prey was transferred from break to talons and he began to call. No response and the mystery deepened. There was no obvious site within easy reach, yet the behaviour was so positive. He took off, and landed on the heavy black plastic netting recently installed on certain stretches of the cliffline to prevent rock falls. Suddenly all was revealed. Instead of taking off again, he dipped his head and squeezed through the wire before disappearing into one of the old jackdaw recesses in the ivy. Seconds later he was out, minus prey, forcing himself through the small square of wire and flying to his favourite perch.

45

The cock kestrel about to land on the wire mesh.

Only with difficulty did the hen kestrel squeeze into the nest hole.

Fulmars constantly discomforted the exiting kestrels.

The Magpie Wood, a typical upland shelter belt in sheep pasture.

The temptation was too great and after a reasonable break to allow the hen to eat the morsel we climbed the cliff and I roped on once more. The squares in the wire may have been big enough for a kestrel, but not for size eight climbing boots, and it was difficult to control the descent. However, the hole was reached with no great mishaps and a surprised kestrel stared back from the sheltered hollow. She slowly retreated off the three eggs and reared to face me, the blood from the recent meal still wet on her beak. A final exchange of glances and I climbed back up at speed. She stayed put. I must admit I had written off the old sites behind the wire. Never underestimate a kestrel.

Woodland, especially blocks of mature sitka spruce, poses particular problems in locating the pairs, let alone the nest sites. Wind-blown areas which have suffered the domino effect can be impossible to penetrate. Even relatively small blocks of shelter-belt timber can be difficult especially if they are unbrashed. Each thick tree top could house a carrion crow's nest.

The Magpie Wood, an isolated plantation in the Waterhead area, was first pencilled in after a chance sighting of a kestrel entering the wood with a vole dangling from its talons. The general area was approached slowly until after a ten minute crawl I was positioned below the calling birds, but the spruce was so thick that no nest could be seen. After climbing four trees without success it was back to the roadside and a patient wait. Half an hour later and the hen flew in, moved slowly along the sitka spruce leaders and dropped straight into the thick crown of a tree near the edge of the area I had searched. The reward — four eggs.

On occasions such as these it is imperative to have back up and on most evenings it is Deirdre Mackinnon, my deputy at Culzean. Having someone stand back and watch at the edge of the wood, while you search or climb, can save valuable time as a bird can sneak off quietly and if you're too close, you may miss it. Deirdre is also very competent in handling the ropes and so far has shown little aspiration for promotion as I'm still in one piece!

I remember vividly at one site, having unsuccessfully clapped and shouted to try and dislodge a hen from a nest somewhere in the ivy on a cliff, I bent down to tie a shoe lace. The hen kestrel chose that moment to fly off and, being alone, it cost me another hour and a half before she came back in and the nest was found. A back up would have spotted the exiting bird.

The sequel to the breeding attempt at the Magpie Wood was quite interesting. The hen eventually completed a clutch of five eggs, hatched four and was given another two chicks to rear. These extra birds had been stolen from a nest in Glasgow, were recovered by the police, reared by Carol Scott from Eaglesham and, finally, fostered back via the nest site at Magpie Wood. Both birds were accepted and fledged under the foster parents. One was recovered in the early winter period at Castle Douglas, 40 kilometres to the south.

A well-tried and very successful method of locating nest sites in large tracts of conifer forest is by the crawl. The Wells is a good example. Mike Callan had located a pair of kestrels in a section of mature sitka about half a kilometre long by a quarter wide. Newly planted ground provided ideal hunting regime all around but the exact nest spot remained a mystery. As usual, the trees were unbrashed and if you were on your knees you could just crawl under the branches. We went to one end of the wood, crawled in under the branches and proceeded to move up and down the length of the block, always keeping each other in sight. All the time our eyes were on the ground looking for the tell-tale pellets, droppings, or the odd feather discarded during preening. The hen begins to moult once she starts incubating. In this instance we were lucky and the debris was spotted after ten minutes. Other times it has taken hours, which can be punishing on the hands and knees. Wet conditions are horrendous. Once the signs are located it's just a case of climbing. Occasionally we pick up antlers cast by red deer stags which use the stands for shelter. In a more open woodland territory it is a case of just wandering slowly up and down, occasionally turning round to gain a different perspective on the tree canopy.

It is essential to conduct these searches, be it in a small or large wood, in complete silence as there is just a chance you will hear the hen calling or the male coming in to give her food. On many occasions we have been alerted by the soft, plaintive call which the hen often makes on the nest if she is a little bit anxious, or is calling her mate. The male will call the female off the nest when he comes in with food, so it's a case of homing in quietly on the noise and observing. The kestrel is not a very vocal bird, but it pays to know the calls and their significance. When alarmed, the kestrel can be extremely noisy and both its common and Latin names are derived from its distinctive, shrill 'kee-kee-kee'.

The Wells:
a kestrel pair is nesting
in that tree line.

Mike Callan crawling along the ditches looking for signs.

Feathers and pellets, the telltale signs.

Once the signs are located it's just a case of climbing.

In these early season forays it is only a matter of time before the sickle-shaped peregrine falcon looms over the skyline to write off another kestrel territory. The kestrel's relationship with the peregrine is such that I have very mixed feelings about the peregrine's presence. I'm sure the Ayrshire situation mirrors what has happened nationally. In the 1970s, the peregrine population gradually began to claw its way back from the brink after the pesticide problems and as the recovery gained momentum so the interaction with the kestrel increased.

There are records of peregrine, raven and kestrel pairs co-existing on the same cliff, but this is certainly not the norm. Prime, traditional territories occupied for centuries by the peregrine had been utilised by kestrels when the decline set in. Inevitably these territories have been repossessed by the peregrine and in most cases in the study areas the kestrel pairs have been displaced. To date, eight of the prime territories have changed tenants causing great hilarity and leg-pulling by members of the S. W. Raptor Group.

What it means in kestrel terms is simply a local movement. The Great Glen, one of the longest sections of rock face in the study areas supported three pairs of kestrels and I ringed 14 young one year within a kilometre distance. Since the peregrine has returned, only one pair of kestrels intermittently nests at the south end of the Glen. In another locality, the most perfect kestrel site for photography was ruined when the local tiercel peregrine chose the nest ledge as a roost. The kestrels deserted a clutch of five eggs. Kestrels too have been well documented among the gull, grouse, pigeon and wader prey items on the plucking posts of the peregrine. When you think of it, a hovering kestrel is a sitting 'duck' to a stooping peregrine.

This first phase of the season serves to get rid of the rust, to become hill fit and regain confidence on cliff faces. In computer terms you become 'kestrel friendly' again and have an early opportunity to gauge what the next few months has in store. For example, on the last day of April 1986, I noted that spring warmth was still well ahead of us. One of the coldest and wettest springs on record had meant hours of frustrating and uncomfortable leg work on territories with hardly a sighting of a kestrel. Only 58 per cent of territories were actually occupied that year, ten pairs did not even lay clutches and it proved a very unproductive year.

The following year conditions were ideal, minimal rainfall and warm weather, and territory occupation reverted to the norm of around 80 per cent. From that base the kestrel population in Ayrshire had one of the most successful seasons since the yearly days of the 1970s. But no matter how good or bad the season, the thrill of the first contact takes some beating:

Diary extract – 31 March 1988:

About 100 metres from the Coastal Cliff site I dropped on to my knees and began the slow, wet crawl to the grassy knoll directly across from the nesting cliff. The atmosphere was perfect, the sun dipping behind the Mull of Kintyre, while the full moon balanced the scales to the east. Very slowly I raised the binoculars above last year's limp grass stems and cautiously scanned the rock face. The hen kestrel was standing on last year's nesting ledge teasing her tail feathers through her beak as she preened. I could even see the ring on her leg. Mission accomplished I edged backwards, eyes never leaving the oblivious bird. Another piece in the jigsaw puzzle and back in the field again.

WHAT'S IN A NAME?

Both the common name, kestrel, and its Latin name, *Falco tinnunculus tinnunculus* (Linnaeus), are derived from the bird's distinctive shrill call 'kee-kee-kee'. The common name comes from the Old French word, *crecele*, probably imitative of the call as the modern French version *crecerelle* means a rattle. Greenoak (1979), Gotch (1981) and Macleod (1954), in their respective books on bird names and lore, are unanimous in attributing *tinnunculus* to the Latin *tinnus* to ring or to scream, yet another reference to the bird's call.

The actual name kestrel appears in the writings of the English naturalist Willoughby (1678) having occurred in Turner (1544) as 'a Kistrel or Kastrel' and in Merrett (1667) as a 'Keshrel or Kastrel'. The two Old English names 'stannel' and 'mushafoe' were overtaken by kestrel probably with the influence of French usage in falconry terms during the Norman period.

Not unnaturally most of the local British names relate to one or other of the bird's characteristic traits, especially hovering. The wind hover (south and west England), the wind cuffer (Orkney) and willy whip the wind (Sussex) are good examples of this. The red hawk (Stirling), maalin (Shetland) and the red kite (Gaelic) refer to its plumage. Mouse hawk (Yorkshire) and mouse falcon (Orkney) refer to the prey of the kestrel, the 'mouse' probably being a general name for small vole-type mammals in the past.

One of the most interesting local names, which again is indicative of the bird's habits, is stannel, from the Old English 'stangale' or 'stone yeller', an obvious reference to the bird calling from rock perches (Yorkshire). A selection of further local and international names are listed below.

Local names of kestrels

Creshawk	Cornwall
Stonegall	
Stand hawk	} Yorkshire
Stannel	
Wind hover	south and west of England
Hoverhawk	Berkshire, Buckinghamshire
Vanner hawk	Sussex
Wind fanner	Surrey

Wind cuffer	Orkney
Wind sucker	Kent
Wind bivver	Sussex
Wind bibber	Kent
Wind hawk	Wales (Cudyll y gwynt)
Red hawk	Stirling, Lancashire
Kite	Shropshire
Keelie	Edinburgh
Maalin	Shetland
Sparrowhawk	Ireland
Blood hawk	Oxfordshire
Field hawk	Surrey
Grasset-hawk	Devon

National names of kestrels

Torenvalk	Holland
Faucon crecarelle	France
Turmfalke	Germany
Cernicalo vulgar	Spain
Tornfalk	Sweden

A full clutch of five eggs in the Limekilns nest hole.

THE FIRST EGG

*T*he first circuit of territories will hopefully have clarified the current year's occupation and the next phase is to locate the exact nest sites being used and record the date when the first egg is laid in each case. This is a key statistic in two ways. Once the first egg is recorded in a cycle then I can timetable the remaining visits for the season to that particular pair with some degree of confidence. Careful planning of the time I have available for fieldwork is critical as the kestrel breeding season of roughly four months is a relatively short one. There is no place for the fair weather fieldworker. Weekly timetables have to be carefully drawn up and adhered to as there is little leeway for recovering lost time. Damp days can have their positive side too as birds tend not to move about as much and hang in at the general nest site area. The second reason is that the timing of the egg laying has an important bearing on the outcome of the season as I'll explain later.

Once a pair has been positively recorded on territory then the location of the nest site is a matter of pride. This is no hard and fast rule but only rarely has the whereabouts of the nest remained a mystery. Some nest sites, like the Dam, Gable End and Limekilns, are used year after year, take no time at all to find and are checked on the initial visit. Others, like the Kenbain situation described previously, may require a few visits before the nest is tracked down. In territories where the kestrels rely upon disused carrion crows' nests, the change of site is more regular as nests deteriorate with age and crumble. A good tip is to spread your net wider when working a wood, pin down the new crows' nests and mark them for the future.

In a day's fieldwork in wooded areas I've calculated that as much as three hours can be spent actually up trees and this is not counting hide work. The ability to climb mature sitka spruce is essential in the Ayrshire study areas, though at times there should be Government Health Warnings on licences: 'Kestrels and Sitka spruce can damage your health'. The use of leg irons to conquer Scots pines is an emergency option only, as I find them very awkward to use.

Some territories can have as many as eight or nine nest sites, any one of which could be used. The Limekilns is a classic example of this, with two sites in the buildings and six to eight in the gully itself. In 1988 kestrels nested on a new ledge at the Limekilns which hadn't been used for certain in the last 15 years, and at Kenbain a carrion crow's nest in a well-hidden crevice nearly beat us. You can never be complacent.

Luck can play its part too. On the first visit to the Magpie Wood one year, I heard a food pass take place and targeted the general area. By the time I'd homed in on the corner of the wood, all was quiet and after 20 fruitless minutes' waiting I decided to climb the tallest tree and look for the nest which was obviously at the top of one of about ten trees. At about 10 metres I glimpsed an outline about five trees away, partly obscured by a branch. A hen kestrel was perched next to a crow's nest, her head bobbing anxiously as she tried to interpret the alien shape. I could even see the single egg in the nest scrape as I was at a higher level. Within seconds she was flying above the wood calling loudly and I left contented.

Kestrels have little architectural skill. They do not build nests and I have no records of nesting material being carried to a potential site. The kestrel's needs are fairly simple – a site which is inaccessible to mammalian predators, adequate shelter from the elements, ease of access to open ground, perches in the vicinity and, ideally, room for limited movement of chicks in the later stages. Of greatest importance is the need for a softish substrate which can be scraped out to form a depression into which the hen can deposit her clutch of eggs. This is done by the bird raking the material with its feet and moulding the depression with its chest. The cup can be as deep as 11 cm although this can vary enormously. The diameter of the scrape varies between 20 and 28 cm. One hen laid her clutch on the bare concrete of the Dam one year but this is a rare occurrence. Often more than one site is scraped by the pair before one is chosen and in the most extreme case a site was scraped 47 days before the first egg was laid.

Some semblance of a nest appears as the cycle progresses when pellet debris, pieces of vegetation nibbled from the immediate vicinity, prey remains and down feathers accumulate both under the eggs and round the rim. The debris which builds up gives the nest site a very distinct aroma.

This inability to construct a nest limits the kestrel in its choice of nest sites, but as long as the substrate allows a scrape they will happily nest on rock ledges, holes in trees, disused nests of other birds, ledges in man-made structures and nest boxes. Nesting on the ground has not yet been recorded in the study areas but one site in boulder scree and another in a rabbit hole on a grassy slope came close. In Ayrshire, there is an abundance of nest sites for kestrels but on saying that, there is a heavy reliance upon old carrion crows' nests in trees.

As one would expect there is a great variety of sites, some well-camouflaged, others quite exposed, like a crow's nest in the top of a spruce tree. Even seasoned campaigners can struggle if the camouflage is good. At one large rock face I stood for an hour while the hen called for the cock bird and failed to find the nest in the ivy. It was another hour before he came in with food and all was revealed. Don Smith, the well-known nature photographer from Darvel, will not mind me telling the story of how he set up a hide at a sparrowhawk's nest, spent many sessions photographing the pair and was completely unaware of a kestrel pair

EGG MATTERS

The bulk of kestrel clutches are laid between mid-April and mid-May but the development of the egg begins much earlier. Work in Holland has shown that the growth of oocytes, the cells which eventually become the eggs, is initiated as early as autumn and continues through winter and spring. The bird's condition, affected by environmental conditions such as food availability, probably dictates the rate of growth. Temperature in spring is also a factor as in cold conditions the bird has less energy available for the formation of eggs.

In species like the kestrel, which lays a clutch over a period of several days, all the yolks grow at the same time but out of phase with each other. The hen kestrel has the ability to store sperm after mating and keep it in a viable condition for days. Experimental work on the American kestrel has shown that a hen is capable of laying fertile eggs two weeks after the last mating. The sperm is stored in special glands and all the eggs could conceivably be fertilised by one mating.

The hen kestrel reduces her activity prior to laying and reduces energy expenditure. The reason for this is that a clutch of five eggs will weigh as much as 120 g, a considerable percentage of her weight, and this is very demanding on the hen. The eggs are laid at one or two-day intervals, normally in the morning.

The egg of the kestrel is blunt and oval in shape with a whitish ground colour which is freely washed and blotched with red-brown. The colour spectrum, even in the same clutch, can be wide — from very dark reddish to almost white. At times the ground colour can be completely masked while conversely pure white clutches are not unknown. Some patterns can be dull, others intricate and very beautiful.

There is no apparent geographical variation in weight and size, though there is naturally a small range in measurements. Eggs weigh between 17 and 22 g and the average size is 39 mm by 31 mm (range 34–44 mm × 28–34 mm).

Clutch size varies from two to seven eggs, though the vast majority of clutches contained between four and six. There is some regional variation in clutch sizes, those in the south of England being slightly smaller than those in the north-east of England and the south of Scotland. If a clutch is lost at an early stage in the cycle a repeat clutch may be laid. Experimental work, again on the American kestrel, demonstrated that kestrel hens were capable of producing over 20 eggs. Ten is the maximum laid by several hens in natural conditions in Ayrshire to date (combining first and repeat clutches).

nesting only 20 metres away. Eventually an adult kestrel was seen carrying a worm into a brood of young kestrels.

Prior to, and during, egg laying is one of the most demanding stages in the cycle as both birds have high energy expenditure. The cock bird takes on the role of provider and brings food to his mate at least a week before the first egg is laid. The hen cuts down on her activity and moves into a state of pre-laying lethargy, rarely leaving the area round the nesting territory. She spends a lot of time perched on or near the site often hunched up with feathers fluffed out and is very reluctant

The hen spends a lot
of time perched on or
near this nest site at the
Limekilns.

A classic clutch of
five eggs on a rock
face nest site.

to leave the spot. In the preceding weeks she has built up large quantities of fat deposits and proteins which go to form the eggs and keep her in good condition through the subsequent period of incubation and brooding.

The reason for the inactivity is not difficult to see as a full clutch of six eggs, laid over a period of eleven days, will weigh 130−40 g, which is almost 50 per cent of her body weight. She requires much more energy than, say, a golden eagle hen which lays a clutch of two eggs, which amounts to only 5 or 6 per cent of her body weight. Eggs are laid at two-day intervals, usually in the morning. The earliest date for laying the first egg I have recorded was on 1 April and the latest on 28 May − both pairs successfully reared young. The circumstances surrounding the finding of the earliest egg were interesting. The hen came off the tree and I was most surprised to find a clutch of five which, on count back, put the date of the first egg at April Fools' Day. The five eggs were sitting in the middle of the crow's nest and the hen's outline was clearly visible due to the hailstones piled round the edge. Despite the atrocious early season conditions the pair reared all five young.

The timing of laying the first egg is an important indicator as to how the pair will fare. Early nesters have a better chance of success and generally rear more young than late nesters. As the season progresses those pairs which start their clutches late tend to lay fewer eggs, have smaller broods and fledge less than the early birds. Young from the earlier breeding attempts also tend to have a better chance of survival after leaving parental care. The reason why early breeders have the edge in both production and survival is that the young fledge at a time of food

The cock bird will relieve the hen for short periods during the day.

THE WEATHER

The weather plays a very important role in the overall outcome of a breeding season. Early or late breeding seasons often coincide with consistent spells of good or bad weather. The emphasis is on the word consistent. In the warm, dry springs of 1981, 1984, 1985 and 1988 in Ayrshire the local kestrels bred early, the majority of first eggs of a clutch being laid in April. Clutch sizes were large averaging 4.9, 5.2, 5.2 and 5.4 respectively.

However, whereas the good weather lasted throughout the 1984 and 1988 seasons and kestrels produced four young per breeding attempt, the weather changed drastically in late spring 1985 and, during one of the wettest and coldest summers on record, the hatching rate and brood survival was poor. Similarly, in 1981, May was very wet and brood sizes were depleted after a good start. In 1983 and 1986 the springs were cold and wet, the kestrels laid very small clutches and production of young was very low.

Warm, dry springs affect positively the density and availability of voles while cold and wet conditions adversely affect both the hunting efficiency and prey availability. Surface activity of voles diminishes when it rains and during downpours kestrels are reluctant to fly and often seek shelter. As the cock bird must provide for himself and his mate from the first stages of the cycle, anything which affects his ability as a provider is important.

Severe weather not only causes problems with food supply which can lead to desertion, it can also destroy nests. Old crows' nests in trees are especially at risk during storms and gales while cliff sites can be washed out. After one particularly inclement spell I climbed a horse-chestnut tree to find the kestrel's eggs floating in a morass of pellets and rainwater. The weather does seem to have most influence at the beginning of the cycle, being one of the factors which determines the timing of laying and consequently the season's productivity. As the season progresses, day length increases allowing more time for hunting, and the food supply also increases as prey populations reproduce as well.

abundance in mid-summer and have a longer period to gain experience and build up reserves before the onset of winter. Breeding numbers and performance are higher in years when warm, dry springs encourage kestrels to nest early and this is discussed in more detail above.

Incubation generally takes 27–29 days for each egg and the majority of hens start to incubate seriously after the laying of the third egg. Incubation is by no means the sole prerogative of the hen and in most pairs where the cycle was observed closely from a hide, the cock bird regularly relieved the hen for periods of up to one hour at a time. The normal pattern is for the cock bird to come into the vicinity of the nest, land on a perch and call to his mate. She will then leave the eggs and take the prey item, often very aggressively, from the cock bird which then flies in and covers the eggs. She devours the prey, preens and comes back in quite quickly. Adults rarely feed at the actual nest site thus preventing the build up of debris which could attract attention. One very agitated cock bird was left in the nest box for two hours one day and it was only his frantic calling which eventually persuaded the hen to return. The hen works the night shift.

A day in the field at this time of year can be stimulating and exhausting.

Diary extract – 20 April 1990:

The target was quite ambitious for a solo trip, ten territories, especially when the Park's five-a-side football competition had rendered me leg weary. Route carefully planned and a note left at the office, I drove down to the first Dam. The sun was shining and the hen kestrel was obviously enjoying the morning warmth as she basked on top of the ladder. Such was her reluctance to leave that I even had the opportunity to check for rings on her legs but she took off before I could be certain. Two cold eggs nestled in the scrape surrounded by a thick layer of pellets. Just the start you want.

Second Dam and a *déjà vu*. The hen was on a ledge outside the nest site and two eggs were in an identical spot. A discarded flight feather spoiled the mirror image. Three siskins were still feeding on the red bag of nuts in the nearby garden and, as I drove to the next Dam, fieldfares were flocking in the fields, obviously held back by the cold, snowy conditions further north.

Dam number three, kestrel hen number three and three eggs. Just to prove

Hen kestrels undertake the bulk of incubation duties.

which type of nest site was in vogue this year, Dam number four had a single egg; the hen kestrel had been feeding on the grassy bank and had been disturbed as I climbed down. This is the first time in eighteen years that all four Dams have been occupied at the same time.

What a difference a few hundred metres makes. Driving into the Quiet Glen, the landscape was completely different – fawns, browns and buffs – the vegetation not even threatening green. The Quiet Glen part of the Waterhead study area had become a marginal constituency over the last few years so hopes were not too high. However, the supporting cast of other wildlife species always makes the journey worth while; sightings of black grouse by the roadside, bubbling curlew and tumbling lapwings, glimpses of roe deer, and dippers scurrying from boulders under the bridge.

Encouragingly, a pair of ravens were nesting in one of the woods so I made a quick exit and concentrated on the old territory.

One less tree to climb as the crow slipped silently off the main nest in the wood. An unusual sight met me at the first nest box. Half an owl's body and tail were sticking out of the box and a tap on the tree trunk verified that it wasn't dead as a quick exit was made. I was totally unprepared for the contents of the box. Little wonder she had been brooding half out of the box. The three owlets, about a week old, were huddled at the front surrounded by piles of dead voles. They were piled up on all sides causing a considerable stench. Six metres up a sitka or not, this had to be recorded. Back to the car for camera and flash unit

The nesting territory in the Quiet Glen.

Black grouse are often encountered on the roadside in the Quiet Glen though numbers are unfortunately decreasing.

Sixty-three short-tailed field voles and two wood mice from the nest box in the Quiet Glen.

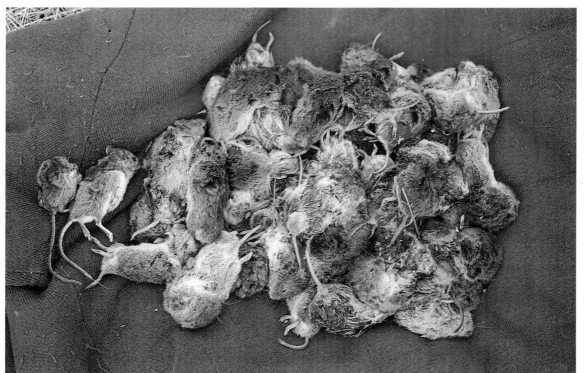

then back up the tree to record the small mammal feast. It wasn't easy as I had to ease back on a couple of branches and hang on by the knees.

Once the photography was completed, I bagged the lot and laid them out on my jacket to count. Incredibly, the final total was 63 short-tailed field voles and two wood mice. The hunting skills of the male must have been phenomenal as the signs of voles in the rough grassland around the wood had not been extensive.

Such a small wood took little time to check and the cock tawny owl was found, in slimline form against the trunk of a sitka at the opposite end of the area. No kestrels and no sign of kestrels. One thing is certain, food shortage is not the reason for non-occupation.

The Magpie Wood was a disappointment. Wind blow had been severe and a quarter of the wood was flattened. A pair of crows and two agitated magpies were the only sightings in an hour-long search, so I proceeded to nearby Waterhead and immediately found a half-eaten vole, a modest offering considering the standards set in the Quiet Glen. The crow's nest in the high sitka had been scraped on the previous visit so up I went. Nothing stirred, but the odd down feather clinging to the rough bark was encouraging. Suddenly, at eye level, she burst from the nest giving me a terrible fright. She had either been asleep or enjoyed brinkmanship. Five eggs were the reward.

I always enjoy the walk up to the Wader Wood as the wet grassland is always inhabited at this time of year by oystercatchers, lapwings, curlew, redshank and, if you're lucky, dunlin. No kestrels in the air and all quiet as I climbed up to the nest box. Another five, warm eggs so she must have slipped off unseen as I entered the wood. Photographic potential noted.

Only the Great Glen left and as soon as I stepped out of the car the powerful silhouette of the peregrine loomed over the cragline. End of story.

As each pair is confirmed as starting to breed so the search begins for the most suitable nest sites which afford opportunities to observe and photograph the cycle from hides. The final choice really comes down to the places where hides can be set up without in any way giving the pair away to other humans. The assortment of structures in which I have sweated and suffered over the years have been at times imaginative and innovative. Others have been torture chambers, requiring a degree of athleticism to which I am unaccustomed. The common denominator is that none have been easy.

Probably the greatest challenge was at the Dam. Once the decision had been taken to join the incubating kestrel on that small platform it was a case of an appropriate design. Endeavouring to simulate a false wall I built a wooden frame the length of the platform, added hardboard sides and painted it as near to the wall colour as possible. It did not survive the climb down to the base of the ladder and was so heavy that manoeuvrability would have been impossible. Back to the drawing board for Mark II, a much superior model with hessian sides and roof, again painted grey to match the walls. This time, after much sweating and cursing it was hauled up the metal ladder and snugly fitted into place. Using a sleeping

The hide in the Dam site shown from above. The nest is behind the ladder.

bag to cushion me from the concrete floor I was able to lie full length with my head only two feet from the incubating hen which accepted the hide as if it had been a permanent fixture. For two seasons I was able to view at close quarters the family life of the breeding pair, so close that your nostrils picked up the smell of the prey items when they were brought in. Emerging from a six-hour spell in the coffin was a painful experience as the limbs required massaging to assist the blood flow. It was a unique situation which I will probably never be able to enjoy again.

My first hide at the Waterhead wood was just as painful at times. The pair had settled for an old crow's nest high in a sitka spruce tree which luckily had a good strong neighbour. A strong whorl of branches afforded a seat almost opposite the nest so a green tarpaulin was tied on to the top of the trunk and spread like a tepee round the top section of the tree. The top of an old broken tripod was lashed firmly to a branch at eye level and I sat on a foam pad in my high-level poncho. If the wind blew, sea sickness was a distinct possibility. Still, the results were reasonable and the cock bird's acceptance of the hide was confirmed when he used it as a roost. On one memorable occasion he flew in to take over the incubation duty and used my head as an intermediate perch before landing on the nest. That's what I call acceptance of a hide.

Having learnt from the previous year when the pair used the nest box in the wood, a new design was attempted which gave a measure of comfort which I richly deserved. At the same height as the previous year a pre-constructed base was battened into position, again at 10 metres. This time a conventional hide was placed on top using four hazel sticks as the corner supports. The luxury of a seat and a tripod made photography so much easier. The reason a pylon was not built was simply because it was a well-frequented wood and would, I'm sure, have been detrimental to the bird's chances of success.

Using the hide, the incubation period can be studied, though, if the truth be told, it is not the most dynamic section of the cycle. For the pair the pace is normally sedate and if the weather is good the cock bird has little difficulty

HIDE DESIGN

The only way really to study the wild kestrel at close quarters is from a hide. Many of the scenarios recounted in this book have been observed through a small opening in a canvas hide positioned for the comfort of both watcher and kestrel. A six-hour session in a cramped space requires concentration and if the body is hurting too much this can detract disastrously from the exercise. For me the ability to move legs and ease cramp is of paramount importance.

Design of a hide and the choice of the most appropriate location near a nest site can make or break a season. Several designs have been effective. The difficulty of locating a hide in an open site, for example where the nest was on a ledge near the lip of a quarry, is overcome by a horizontal design. Six, 60 cm-long stakes were hammered into the ground on the opposite rim to the nest and a green tarpaulin was laid on top. It was then a case of lying on a sleeping bag and working in great comfort. In this case, as in many others, the key to the operation was not hiding from the bird, but making sure that the structure was not obvious to the human eye. The simulated wall design described on page 64 for use at the Dam was a similar example of camouflage design.

A tree site at a height of six or more metres can cause great problems. A tower is easily the best way to overcome the height problem especially if there are no other trees conveniently placed nearby but the very size of the construction can both advertise and give easy access to an intruder. Two methods of overcoming the tree problem have proved successful. The tepee design is the simplest, but can also be the least stable and most demanding on the flesh. A tarpaulin is wrapped round the chosen tree and tied at the top. A seat, like a child's swing, is then suspended inside the tent-shape and a sturdy wooden frame fixed to the tree to hold the tripod. This type of hide is a quick method for observation and is easy to camouflage at the end of a recording session as you simply wrap it round the tree trunk and tie it up.

The most effective design is to use a base with a conventional box hide on top. A simple design is illustrated in Figure 3. The base must be supported on a couple of strong branches to supplement the bolts which hold the structure to the tree trunk. A hole in each corner of the base will take the four main braces for the hide and the top corners can be tied to the nearest branches.

Acceptance of the hide by the kestrel pair is naturally the main concern, allied to the need for keeping the site secret. The ethics associated with working at close quarters with any wild bird are well documented in most wildlife photography books.

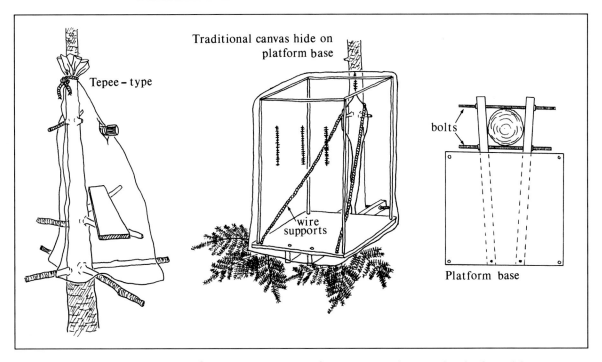

Tepee – type

Traditional canvas hide on
platform base

wire
supports

bolts

Platform base

*Figure 3
Hide designs.*

supporting his mate. As you watch it is easy to slip into the rhythm of the moment. Once the initial disturbance is over it is amazing how quickly the bird will settle and photographic opportunities are limited. The birds soon become accustomed to the hide and will even ignore the odd noise or movement. Two incidents spring to mind which illustrate just how brazen a hen can be.

A sheer-sided open quarry had provided an excellent opportunity for photography as the pair had chosen a ledge high up on the face which was in good light for most of the day. The problem was to design a hide which didn't stick out like a sore thumb. Eventually six 60 cm stakes were driven into the top of the quarry edge about 6 metres across from the ledge and this served to prop up a piece of green tarpaulin which was pegged down with large stones. To watch the nest you crawled in the back and lay prone on your stomach and had an excellent, comfortable view of the pair. After only two sessions the hen became completely indifferent to my approach and if you moved in slowly it was easy to get in and out without her batting an eyelid.

Another hen just would not budge when it rained.

Diary extract – The Waterfall, June 1986:

The drive to the Waterfall site had been in glorious sunshine but when we reached the hills the heavens opened. Having made the effort we decided to at least carry the components of the hide and leave them as near to the nest as possible. The Waterfall is yet another special place. Picture a small waterfall with well-vegetated cliffs on both sides and a dark peaty pool below. A sitka forest was growing up around the site but the trees were planted well back from the stream and the territory still had an open feel about it.

As we carried the poles and canvas down through the lines of trees the sodden ground absorbed any sound and we carefully moved to a small knoll to survey the scene. The hen was sitting on a clutch of eggs on a ledge about 30 metres away and made no effort whatsoever to move. Slowly we edged our way in until we were in the exact position to erect the hide. Still she sat and watched us, not even raising herself off the eggs when a dipper sped downstream. We carefully laid the poles down, piled the canvas on top and stuck a coke can at the edge to get the bird used to a lens substitute. Backing off slowly we left the sodden single-minded hen in the knowledge that the eggs were in good hands.

As I said, the incubation period is relatively sedate. Apart from turning the eggs at regular intervals the hen is continually changing her position while incubating and, although prone to dozing in hot weather, she normally remains in a state of alert, responding to any sign of a change in her surroundings by inclining her head or rising off the eggs. I did on one occasion climb a sycamore tree to inspect a clutch thinking the hen was away, only to find her asleep in the nest hole. She was left in peace despite the temptation to catch and ring her. She was the exception rather than the rule.

The hen starts to moult at the onset of incubation and her feathers are added to the nest debris. In the case of the Waterhead bird in 1986, which sat unsuccessfully on a clutch of five eggs for a record 77 days, the nest box rim was lined with her cast offs. Her vigil had a dramatic end.

Diary extract – Waterhead, 16 July 1986:

The wood was very quite though the floor had been churned by cattle which had been released on to the hill. As I started to climb the tree, incredibly she came off the box. The rest of the branches were taken in a rush until I was peering into the box which still contained two eggs, almost submerged in a morass of mutilated feathers and pellets. There was evidence of two smashed eggs on the landing board and it was no great dilemma to remove the eggs and release the loyal pair. Retribution was swift as the eggs shattered on handling. Deirdre could smell the resultant fumes 10 metres below. Even the midges evacuated the area and my descent broke all records!

The next job was to dismantle the hide and supporting platform. Unfortunately, the midges had all gathered on this particular tree to discuss the 77-day-old eggs because the carnage they caused produced massive lumps on protected and unprotected parts. The kestrel kept well away but the crows put in an appearance to satisfy their curiosity. Twenty-five minutes of purgatory before the hide was down and we were able to beat a hasty retreat.

The habit of nibbling at vegetation has already been mentioned and the birds have also been seen heaping up the nest rim with such material presumably to build up a more effective buffer for the eggs when the hen leaves in a hurry. Eggs can easily be dislodged. While not attempting to give kestrels human attributes there is little doubt that hens do get bored and will, on very hot days, move off the eggs and perch on the edge of the nest or on a nearby perch knowing that the eggs are in no danger of chilling. By the end of the incubation period the eggs can often be stained and dirty, especially if the weather has been inclement.

The only time she leaves the nest other than at a food change is when an intruder appears. If it is an avian enemy, like a crow or magpie, she calls in the male and will join him in mobbing and chasing off the intruder. The hen's reactions to a human varies a lot, with some hens sitting tight until the last minute before launching themselves off the nest and zigzagging away using an evasive flight pattern. On most occasions they circle the nest site in a wide arc calling loudly, but one or two bold individuals have come in very close and twice I've been clipped by the wing tips of adventurous hens.

Collecting the third vital piece of information, the clutch size is not too difficult as most of the nest sites have been pinpointed and it is usually a case of racing round four or five territories in an evening. I need a sample of about 30 clutch sizes each year to allow a good comparison with previous seasons. For a flavour of one of these evenings let's go back to 7 May 1987.

Diary extract – 7 May 1987, 'Four Out of Five':

The Culzean football team had just pulled off a 5–1 victory against the 'auld enemy', Threave Gardens, the only other National Trust for Scotland property able to raise 11 men, so Mike Callan and I decided to check five territories on the way home. We both moved like geriatrics as we gingerly climbed down the rocks to the base of the Dam.

It was a warm, calm evening and we'd picked up the cock kestrel sunning himself on the ledge outside the nest. He slipped over the top of the dam as soon as the car door shut. As we hobbled along the dried-out watercourse the barn owl flew out of the valve unit and floated across to the cover of the hanging beech wood. A barn owl in flight must be one of the most beautiful and evocative sights in the natural world.

The hen kestrel, obviously alerted by the cock bird's departure, silently vacated the nest site as we began to climb. Both of us made heavy weather of the climb but the clutch of five eggs took all our attention. There had been two scrapes earlier and the curious thing was that they both had held single eggs. Now only one was being used and by scraping away the pellet debris in the second cup we found the other egg, intact, but buried about an inch below the surface. Satisfied we left and by the time we were back at the car the hen was on the ledge ready to cover the eggs once the intrusion was over.

Passing the shepherd on the way in, we found Waterhead very quiet and she only came out of the box when I was half way up the tree. She had completed her clutch adding two more to the four recorded on an earlier visit. Already she was well into the moult. We were on a good run so just for good measure we walked the wood putting up a long-eared owl and finding a carrion crow on five newly hatched young.

As we pulled up at the Magpie Wood, a curlew was desperately mobbing a local crow and Mike volunteered to do the climbing – at last. She came off and his jubilant cry confirmed that once more we had a six, again in a nest box.

The next wood, now christened the Ram Wood due to the splendid male sheep which grazed the area, was similarly quiet and as we crept through the trees nothing stirred. In the small clearing just below the nest box, the sight of a newly plucked vole looked promising. We had not been quiet enough as the hen kestrel was on the edge of the box, but, instead of disappearing, she just peered down at us occasionally bobbing her head to refocus. Out came the cameras but the enclosed canopy foiled any photography. We discussed the situation but she merely kept her beady eyes on us. Finally I decided to climb up and much to Mike's amusement she responded by craning her neck to get a better view of a sweating naturalist. She finally decided that discretion was the better part of valour and almost nonchalantly flew off. No need to guess the clutch size, another magnificent six, further confirmation of a good season in prospect.

One last wood, almost a carbon copy of the last three, and finally our luck ran out. Mike undertook the climb up to a nest box in the top of yet another sitka but only one egg was present. It was pale in colour, lacking the rich mottled background of the normal kestrel egg. Once more the decision was easy as, after three weeks and being stone cold, the chances of the breeding attempt continuing in that box were slim, so the egg was removed. If only all the evenings were like this!

The echo of the last sentence brings back very negative memories of spring 1986. It was 8 May before I saw my first egg that year after more than a month of constant fieldwork in atrocious conditions. Rain, wind and a chill, penetrating wind were constant companions as each territory was methodically checked to no avail. Those kestrels which were about were lying low.

However, there are always cameos to keep the pot boiling in any season.

Diary extract – Limekilns, 16 May:

I crawled to a vantage point about 50 metres from the Limekilns face and surveyed the two potential nest holes through the binoculars. Of the two entrances the one on the right looked the part as the vegetation was flattened. Even if the bird was present it could not be seen as the scrape was well back in the cavity. Deciding not to use the rope, I slowly heaved my way up the stone wall and looked in. The hen kestrel rose off a clutch of five eggs and stood glaring at me, eyeball to eyeball. The encounter was brief as she rushed to escape. I offered no resistance, flattened myself against the wall and held on grimly as she sped off.

UNDER PRESSURE

Most research work on kestrel populations has shown that the bulk of breeding failures occur at the pre-laying stages of the cycle. The Ayrshire data is no different with 26 per cent of failures happening before an egg was laid and 57 per cent at the clutch stage. The four main causes of failure were human interference (40 per cent), competition or predation from other avian species (20 per cent), desertion associated with adverse weather conditions (20 per cent) and natural accidents (6 per cent). In the remaining 14 per cent of failures the reason could not be positively determined.

The high instance of human interference in Ayrshire is lower than in south-east and eastern England and London and is caused in the main by children stealing clutches for small collections. Traditional cliff sites within cycling or walking distance of centres of population like towns and villages are most vulnerable. Not being a rare raptor the kestrel tends not to fall victim to the professional oologist.

Persecution by gamekeepers is much less of a problem than in the past but, alas, it still goes on. One keeper did admit to shooting a kestrel at the nest when he was doing his rounds of crows' nests with the shotgun. This kind of accident must happen occasionally as the kestrel does utilise this type of nest site extensively in Ayrshire. The kestrel's relative innocence with regard to the taking of game birds as prey was recognised by Mackie in *The Keeper's Book* in 1877:

> Still I do not advocate the destruction of this beautiful bird. Let the keeper find the nest, watch what is brought to it, and use his judgement as to whether or not the death warrant shall be pronounced.

Kestrels will take very young game birds soon after they hatch if they are readily available and odd rogues will return regularly to rearing fields to reap an easy harvest. In the same book another passage illustrates the classic 'plant':

> That distinguished naturalist, the late Duke of Argyll instructed his

keepers not to kill kestrels as they were harmless to game. His Grace however changed his mind on the Head Keeper's showing him remains of many grouse at a kestrel's nest.

It is incredible that in the latter part of the twentieth century we still have over a third of kestrel breeding failures being attributed to direct, deliberate interference by human beings. To people working with birds of prey it is a source of intense frustration and despite sterling efforts by the RSPB the illegal practices still continue in many large estates.

Remaining objective is much easier when recording natural disasters like failures due to weather conditions, accidents and competition with other species. I find the interaction between the kestrel and other species of raptors one of the most fascinating aspects of the work. Just when you think you're clear in your head about the relationship between two species one individual pair will blow a generalisation. The barn owl is a classic example.

Up until 1988 I would have said that the barn owl and the kestrel live quite happily together and there is little interaction. The evidence for this was the numerous shared territories and instances of nesting very close together. Such was the frequency of this that Ian Leach, who worked on the barn owl in Ayrshire for several years, and I swapped a lot of information and saved a considerable amount of time in the field.

One of the most interesting shared sites was a disused farmhouse miles from anywhere in the hills. Ian had located barn owls which were nesting on the floor behind the door in the toilet upstairs. The kestrels were 'downstairs' in the porch on a ledge above the door. On one joint expedition to ring the young kestrels and catch the adult owls we were in the loft when we heard an irregular banging sound. The historical association between ghost stories and barn owls is heightened when you're in a pitch-black, vile-smelling loft holding one of these beautiful but equally smelly birds. The bird was processed – ringed, weighed and measured – and still the knocking persisted. Very gingerly we searched the building, gradually homing in on the sound. Would you believe a lamb with a tin can jammed over its head blindly walking into the steading walls? The laughter was as much relief as anything else.

Yet others nested together in an open-sided hay shed, the kestrel on a ledge at the top of the bales while the barn owl was in a hole lower down. Memories of a photographic session at this site are of the incredible cacophony of hisses, squeaks and snores from the owl family at dusk. Both pairs reared five young. I also have records of pairs nesting in different ledges in the same rock face and it came as quite a surprise when the owls began to take an interest at the Dams.

On the first visit of 1988 to the Dams a pair of barn owls was obviously in residence in one dam but the kestrels were hanging about the second structure though it also showed recent signs of barn owl roosting. Things progressed normally and on the second visit a kestrel egg was found in the scrape and both birds were seen.

Visit number three was illuminating. The four kestrel eggs in the clutch

THE BARN OWL

The barn owl is the kestrel's nocturnal counterpart, not only choosing similar territories and prey populations, but sometimes accommodation as well. However, the fortunes of the successful kestrel are in marked contrast to the barn owl, which has declined over much of Britain to the present population of approximately 5,000 breeding pairs. Reasons for the decline include the use of pesticides, changes in farming practice, loss of habitat and nest sites, and the use of poison for vermin control.

Recent research has pinpointed certain key trends. Winter mortality has increased significantly as winters have become more severe in the last 50 years. It has been estimated that starvation occurs and the population drops dramatically if snow cover exceeds 20 days. This has happened in 21 winters since 1940.

Removal of hedges, grassland, ditches, woodland and wetland from farmland has also taken its toll as the barn owl is essentially a bird of edges and margins, hunting in the rough grassland associated with these habitat types. The reduction in the number of wildlife-rich hay fields in favour of silage crops, and the disappearance of hay ricks and their rats, mice and small birds have adversely altered the availability of certain prey. Research work in south-west Scotland has indicated that a pair of barn owls require 8−10 kilometres of woodland edge in their territory to keep the breeding performance high enough to maintain a stable population.

Heavy mortality caused by collisions on roadsides, which often harbour the only rough grassland verges in a district, could be as high as 5,000 individuals killed per year countrywide, and this would account for one youngster from every brood. When populations are as small as the barn owls' these statistics become extremely significant.

In Ayrshire, the situation seems typical of many areas in the country. Barn owl pairs have become scarcer despite the relative abundance of nest sites and an adequate food supply. Small pockets of two or three pairs are the norm now and this very isolation may work against the species as linking grassland corridors become fewer, hampering the interchange of birds.

A barn owl arriving at the nest hole.

The 'upstairs' nest of the barn owl in the toilet of the derelict cottage.

were cool and in a second scrape only a few centimetres away were two white eggs. Four or five decapitated voles were tucked in at the wall. There was no sign of either kestrels or barn owls. By visit number four, there were four kestrel eggs and five barn owl eggs in the same scrape and it was a barn owl which vacated the platform as I climbed up. The barn owl continued to incubate the nine eggs and each visit was eagerly awaited. Sadly, the kestrel eggs did not hatch, and when they were examined showed only the very early stages of embryonic growth. Presumably during the period when the takeover took place the eggs had been uncovered for several days and the chilly nights had proved fatal. Five owlets hatched and were successfully reared.

The kestrels were easily tracked down to the nearby quarry, also used by the cock barn owl for roosting, and, after a gap of two weeks, settled down, the hen laying five eggs and rearing the full complement. This takeover was not an isolated case. In 1989 one pair of barn owls started to roost in the tower of one of the dam sites and I assumed it was just a winter roost for the inhabitants of an old ruined tower a mile away. Not so, not only did they decide to nest but they used my hide, which had served so well to photograph kestrels, for the scrape. On a later visit I found a clutch of four kestrel eggs behind the ladder. This was followed by a clutch of seven eggs laid by the barn owl in the old hide. The two clutches were less than a metre apart and almost inevitably the kestrel was moved out by the owl and the eggs smashed. Once more the kestrel pair moved about 400 metres away and successfully nested on a ledge in the quarry.

Despite these incidents and instances of food piracy (see page 76), the barn owl and kestrel tend to co-habit quite readily, which is not usually the case with the tawny owl.

Tawny owls do compete for the same nest sites as kestrels and regularly break up a sequence of kestrel breeding attempts. One such territory exists on the coastal cliffs at Culzean. The much sought after nest hole is in a recess on an ivy-covered sandstone face which can be checked by crawling along a precarious ledge (not one of Mike Callan's favourites). In 1988 I watched the kestrel pair for two weeks as they settled down on the territory and stood only metres away from the hen as she called her mate on to the ledge. A week later the kestrels were gone and the tawny owl was sitting on two eggs.

Several years earlier, I had patiently followed the kestrel pair's progress to the point where two eggs had been laid. Not wishing to risk overdisturbing the only kestrel pair in the Park that year I didn't go back for about two weeks. Peering into the nest after the controlled absence I counted four eggs, two of which were slightly larger, whiter and less elliptical than the normal kestrel egg. A kestrel had been seen above the cliffs as I approached but no bird came out of the nest hole. Imagine my surprise, and I must admit disgust, when on the next visit a tawny owl flew out leaving a newly hatched owlet among the pellets and the other whitish egg. The kestrel eggs were found lying at the back of the cavity, stone cold. Both owlets hatched, the older chick ate the younger chick and the net result was one more tawny owl in the Park at the end of the season.

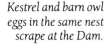

Kestrel and barn owl eggs in the same nest scrape at the Dam.

This particular site seems to have all the ingredients for both tawny owls and kestrels and the competition seems to be an annual one as incidents like the one described below are commonplace.

Diary extract — The Craigs, 14 April 1988:

The first willow warbler was in song as I walked along the beach to the base of the cliff and no sooner had I begun the climb than a hen kestrel left the ledge and landed on a nearby tree. Unconcerned, she sat staring down at me. After a couple of minutes I moved up and she lazily moved along to a more distant perch.

FOOD PIRACY AND THE KESTREL

A number of food piracy records have been published over the years concerning birds of prey, and the kestrel has been cited as both aggressor and victim. The normal circumstance is of a bird on the ground in possession of an item of prey being attacked and displaced. A typical example is of a short-eared owl flying back to its territory carrying a vole and landing near the nest site. As it passed the food item from foot to beak, a cock kestrel dived in, grabbed the prey and fled. The owl gave chase but quickly broke off, being unable to keep up with the speed of the thief.

Kestrels have also been seen pirating food from sparrowhawks, merlins, long-eared owls and barn owls. One audacious, if not suicidal, kestrel snatched a chaffinch from a peregrine after the song bird had been cornered in a bush. The peregrine did not pursue.

While many of these robberies must be opportunistic, there is a record of one kestrel preying on a particular barn owl. The kestrel, a cock bird, was observed, sitting on a chicken coop in a small field, calling loudly. Suddenly, a barn owl flew out of the coop carrying a small rodent towards the nearby barn. The kestrel gave chase and attacked the owl from behind, grabbed the rodent and appeared to be 'back-pedalling'. The owl continued flying, dragging the kestrel behind it and both birds disappeared into the barn still locked together. Neither bird was seen for half an hour, then the kestrel was spotted preening in a tree.

In the afternoon the observers returned to the same spot to find the barn owl quartering the field. It successfully caught a rodent and mantled it in the grass. Within seconds, the kestrel appeared from nowhere and landed on the owl's back. They rolled over in the grass fighting for the prey which the kestrel wrestled from the unfortunate owl and made off. The barn owl lay in the grass for about a minute then resumed hunting. When it next caught a small rodent it wisely swallowed it immediately

Far from always being the aggressor, the kestrel does suffer from the attentions of other raptors and has been seen losing out to red-footed falcons, barn and short-eared owls. Kestrels will also tackle other kestrels especially when hunting territories overlap.

Tawny owls compete vigorously with kestrels for nest sites.

To reach the three potential nest holes, I needed to crawl along a sandstone ledge of dubious strength using the ivy as hand grips. Unexpectedly a tawny owl burst from the ivy and disappeared along the cliff pursued by agitated chaffinches and blue tits. Edging slowly along to the last recess I found four, white owl eggs deep in the ivy. Turning to struggle back I was suddenly aware of rapid wing beats and instinctively flattened myself against the cliff face. The reputation of tawny owls demanded instant respect. Once more it was a case of wrong bird. Glancing up after the 'whoosh' I saw, and then heard, an irate cock kestrel gaining height after the attack.

Thankfully he was satisfied with his first sortie and contented himself with calling loudly from the cliff top as I scrambled back. Safely back on terra firma I watched the pair for ten minutes as first the hen joined him on the grassy banking, then they mated. Surely this year the kestrels will breed in the Park after an absence of several years.

The sequel to this was that the kestrel pair moved to the very edge of the territory and reared three young on a similar, ivy-covered, coastal cliff face. In 1990 the kestrels and tawny owls both reared young on the ledge, the two holes being only 45 cm apart. You can never take anything for granted.

Only one positive interaction with the long-eared owl was recorded during the past 18 years. Kestrels had bred successfully in a mature Scots pine plantation for many years and the pair had been seen prospecting a crow's nest early in the season. The second visit to check the egg-laying date was made with some confidence. The tree was a typical Scots pine, no branches for the first four metres, and as soon as the climb began a long-eared owl flew off the nest. Two white eggs were confirmed and a search revealed the remains of a kestrel hen on the ground not far from the base of the tree. Chewed quills confirmed the work of a fox. The possible interpretation was that the hen kestrel had been injured in a struggle with the owl for the nest site and the injured bird had been taken by a prowling fox. I leave it to your imagination for a solution. Certainly the two species nest quite readily in the same small woods and normally rear young successfully.

We have already seen how the peregrine falcon recovery has had some effect on the kestrel population in Ayrshire. Unfortunately the same encouraging picture cannot be painted for the diminutive merlin. Numbers of merlin breeding pairs in Ayrshire are low. Despite painstakingly searching huge areas of ideal habitat each year Dick Roxburgh, the raptor co-ordinator, and his team usually locate only around a dozen pairs. This decline is nationwide and is very worrying at a time when optimistic trends are being recorded for the majority of raptor species in Britain. The loss of heather moor habitat and favoured low to mid-hill ground to the sitka revolution has added to the problems of pesticides and persecution. Competition from the more powerful sparrowhawk, a beneficiary of the new afforestation, is yet another problem as is the fact that the speedy merlin, which uses the lowest air space when hunting, is the most accident prone of our birds of prey.

This merlin hen was brooding young only 50 metres from the kestrel site.

Merlins in Ayrshire nest on the ground and in crows' nests and with such a wealth of sites available there is little conflict between them and the kestrel. In fact, kestrels will tolerate merlins as close neighbours and this saved one brood of the smallest falcons from certain death. On a tract of heavily keepered moor a kestrel pair nested in a crow's nest behind a rowan tree in a cleugh, while the merlins nested on the heather bank thirty metres upstream. The keeper blasted the young kestrels and shot one of the adults but did not investigate further, assuming that he'd removed all the 'vermin' from the vicinity. Four young merlins managed to run the gauntlet and enrich the moors with their presence. In truth, with the population at such a low ebb, they cannot possibly be seen as competitors of the ubiquitous kestrel.

Sparrowhawks and kestrels, the commonest raptors in Ayrshire, interact but rarely compete for nest sites or food, though the remains of one young kestrel were found on a sparrowhawk plucking post. Hen harriers and golden eagles are regrettably scarce in the south-west of Scotland and likewise pose few problems. The bird which causes the kestrel most annoyance is clearly the carrion crow and their aerial battles are a daily occurrence during the breeding season. Given the chance, an unguarded clutch will be quickly pilfered by the wily corvids.

When accidents do occur it tends to be when the kestrels nest in old crows' nests. The nests do not last for ever and on several occasions clutches have been found on the ground below collapsed structures. Wood cutting operations also account for some nest failures but these are not deliberate acts.

However, despite the ravages of the weather, the unneighbourly behaviour of near relatives, the irrational behaviour of human beings and Acts of God — the incubation period for the majority of kestrel breeding pairs is not a taxing experience. By the middle of May the season is well underway and the third vital piece of information, clutch size, has been safely recorded.

Before release, the feather condition of the Gable End Cock bird is assessed.

CLOSE ENCOUNTERS

*T*here are still two very important tasks which I must complete before chicks begin to hatch. The first is to make a final sweep of all the territories assessed as unoccupied in the early part of the season to double check that no pairs have been missed. This can happen, especially when a pair starts to breed later than the rest of the population, or if a pair use a new site on the periphery of the territory, well away from the normal haunts.

One classic case was at the tawny owl cliff site described in the last chapter. The kestrels had been thwarted in their attempts to breed at one site and despite seeing the birds regularly it was with acute embarrassment that the pair were finally found nesting – on the cliff below my office! In mitigation I would plead that the birds were very silent and the site itself was unusual as it was enclosed by trees.

Kenbain in 1988 was the site of another late pair which very nearly slipped through the net. Several visits were made but only an odd sighting had been recorded and a well-scraped nest ledge on a cliff section had not borne fruit. I decided to make one last visit and work up the coast from the southern extremity of the territory. Parking the car proved to be inspirational. The noise of the car door closing put the jackdaws off the cliffs accompanied by a hen kestrel. Intrigued, Deirdre and I walked over to the base of the cliff but could not see any signs and after ten minutes left to search the rest of the coastline.

It proved to be a fruitless exercise but mindful of the initial sighting of the evening we approached the rock buttress back at the car with extreme caution. Deirdre stood well back from the face while I moved in closer. Between us we had total visual coverage. At a given signal we both clapped loudly – and the hen kestrel obligingly left a deep cleft which on closer inspection harboured a precariously balanced stick nest.

There was no possible way of climbing directly to the site up the sheer wall of lava and an overhang prevented examination from above. Eventually after lengthy debate I climbed the face to the right and, directed by Deirdre, edged my way along a ledge to within five metres of the nest. The reward for running the gauntlet of irate fulmars spitting their foul oily mixture was five kestrel eggs nestling among the sticks. We shall hear more of this nesting attempt later.

Another pair in 1988 which almost eluded me was the Magpie Wood territory. Three visits, nest box untouched and not even a sighting. On the last day in April I decided on an eight-territory blitz and after a bonus in the Great Glen, where a pair had defied the peregrines and laid two eggs, and a complete blank at Waterhead, I arrived at a very silent Magpie Wood. A binocular scan from the car did little to raise hopes. Long-eared owl pellets littered the woodland edge and I moved quietly to the tree which housed the box. The climb too was in vain, the base showing no signs of use. Deciding to stand for half an hour as a last gesture, I was only minutes into the vigil when a kestrel began calling softly from a thick stand of high sitka about 30 metres away.

The hunting instinct took over and for the next hour I moved at snail's pace towards the sound, stopping for ten-minute periods to make sure that this unexpected bonus wasn't blown. She was definitely unaware of my presence despite the alarm call of a wren which insisted on following my progress and giving vent to its irritation. In the closely packed trees my only hope was to remain incognito and hope for a change over. At last I was below what must be the site but no crow's nest could be seen in the dense top branches. Unwilling to climb the tree I settled down to sit it out. Fifteen minutes passed without incident until the silence was broken by the cock bird's arrival and greeting calls. Off she came and the tree was confirmed. A quick climb revealed a full clutch of six and it had all been worth while.

One territory near the Coastal Cliff proved to be incredibly well hidden. Deirdre had found the pair late and I abseiled off the hundred foot cliff and stopped at the ledge which she'd assured me housed the nest. Absolutely no sign of any kestrel activity. I completed the abseil and confronted a disbelieving Deirdre. We decided to withdraw to a vantage point several hundred metres away and, incredibly, the hen kestrel flew into the exact ledge and disappeared. Down I went again, the hen came off, but when I reached the spot I still couldn't find any sign. I tied myself off and hung there puzzled and frustrated. After a few minutes I heard a very faint cheeping noise and could hardly believe it when the site was eventually located. The crack in the rock was only 8 cm wide and all that was visible from the face view was a dark line. The bird had to fly straight into what looked like a solid face then take a sharp right turn. Consequently there was no outward sign of an entrance. Six newly hatched young were confirmed by touch only.

Each season without fail at least one late pair is located on the late sweep so thoroughness usually pays dividends. Rarely a pair can slip through the net. By far the most confusing situation I've ever encountered was in a shelter belt adjacent to hundreds of acres of prime, vole-infested, young conifers. An early visit had been straightforward, two eggs in a nest box on the ege of the wood. The second visit was slightly disconcerting as three kestrels, two hens and a cock, were in the airspace above the trees. After checking the nest box and confirming five eggs, I settled down in the wood to await developments. The reward was confusion.

I heard at least two sets of kestrels in different parts of the wood and, for the next three weeks, hours of fieldwork failed to unravel the mystery.

Endless climbing of trees revealed one scraped kestrel site, two tawny owls' nests with five young in each, a pair of long-eared owls and various combinations of kestrels above the wood, five being the maximum. The feeding must have been phenomenal to support such a high density of birds of prey and the general level of activity at any time was fascinating to watch and listen to. Sadly the kestrel pair using the box deserted for reasons unknown, but a second pair were located one hundred metres away. By this time they were too large to ring and, as I climbed the tree to investigate, all five took to the air. I still, to this day, believe that a third pair was located in the wood.

Although I stick mainly to the prescribed sample territories, I regularly explore new ground, often in response to a telephone call from one of the contacts and often in areas adjacent to existing study plots. One of the delights of working with kestrels is that they provide such a good excuse for pottering in glens, woods and derelict buildings.

There is little doubt that one of the most exciting tasks carried out is catching adult kestrels to study their fidelity to nesting territories. It is necessary to catch the birds as it is almost impossible to identify individuals in the field unless they have some unusual marking or deformity. This is done during the incubation period once the birds are settled into a routine. I was initiated into this aspect of raptor research work by Andy Village in 1979 at Eskdalemuir in south Scotland, a place best known for its horrendously high rainfall. Under the supervision of Ronnie Rose, the Wildlife Manager of the Economic Forestry Group's well-designed plantations in the area, Andy had a good sized population of kestrels under observation. Using a technique, well-tried in the USA, he caught a sample of adult kestrels each year.

Details of the trapping method are naturally not a matter for open discussion but suffice to say that it works very well and in no way damages the birds or affects its breeding performance. The training day not only reassured me but also gave valuable practice and experience in handling adult kestrels. Armed with a special licence from the Nature Conservancy Council (which incidentally forbids discussion of the trapping method) I began to trap at selected territories from 1980 onwards.

Nonetheless, training or no, it was with some trepidation that I attempted my first trapping. I chose a territory which had an excellent record of success for kestrels over the years and in the company of Don Smith we set off for the Stables. Set in a typical lowland estate, this territory has a familiar blend of woodland, farmland and scrub habitats. The kestrel pair normally nest in one of the myriad holes in the masonry of a derelict stable complex, but in 1980 the alternative site, a hole high in a mature horse-chestnut had been chosen. I climbed the tree to see if she was incubating and before I was half-way up she left a clutch of six and circled the wood. Trap set we retired to the vehicle to await developments. Dense cover prevented us from keeping an eye on the trap but she was spotted returning to the general vicinity of the nesting tree a few minutes after we left. Determined not to spoil the first attempt by being over eager, we curbed the natural instinct to take an occasional peep at the trap, and gave her a chance to become statistic number one.

Twenty long minutes elapsed until finally we capitulated and literally ran back through the wood. She was caught and the surge of adrenalin was incredible. She was quickly released from the trap and, even before admiring her, a ring was fixed to her leg just in case she inadvertently broke free. Far from succumbing gently to all this attention she struggled fiercely, lashing out with lethal talons. Very firm handling was needed to avoid damage to myself and her. The technique used to immobilise the bird was to pin the wings close to the body and, with the legs held straight down the length of the tail, encircle the lower half of the body with one hand − just like the pigeon fancier's grip. It was imperative to put the legs out of commission as the talons can do more damage than the beak.

We relaxed once she was ringed and under control and were able to inspect a breeding adult at close quarters. She was in very good condition, her feathers were not ragged at the edges and she had barely begun to moult. Pale in colour, she was nonetheless boldly marked and certainly not a first year bird. By pinching her breast muscles we ascertained that she was quite plump and obviously not lacking in resources. This was further confirmed when she was placed in a bag and weighed using a small balance. Three hundred grams exactly, which is a good middle weight for a hen kestrel.

One very obvious feature was her brood patch which was easily revealed by blowing back the lower breast feathers. This bare patch of skin, which is well supplied with blood vessels, comes into direct contact with the eggs as she incubates and is an important source of heat. The patch is formed when the hen loses feathers as she begins the laying process.

Mindful of the time she was off the clutch, the inspection was not prolonged and we took her to a point well away from where she had been handled for release. This was to ensure that the bird did not associate the catching and subsequent handling by humans with the breeding site and possibly cause desertion. Thankfully she zigzagged off and, after circling the wood for a minute, she dropped out of sight. The uncertainty of the operation was not eased until two days later when Don phoned to report that a return visit to the nest site had confirmed that all was well.

From that successful springboard I have endeavoured to catch up to 15 adults each season in selected, traditional territories like the Dams, Kenbain, and the Limekilns. The great advantage that catching and ringing adults has over ringing chicks is that if successful you are presented with an immediate answer. The adult you have in your hand has either been ringed by you or someone else as a chick or an adult, or is unringed with previous history unknown. Regardless, you have the information at once and don't have a long wait for the British Trust for Ornithology printout which tells you that a chick you ringed at the Crumbling Quarry has been found dead by a roadside in Holland at the age of four years.

What is emerging from the catching programme is evidence of a rapid turnover of adults at the selected territories with only one real exception, that being the first hen caught at the Stables. She was caught at the same nesting territory for

The kestrel hen's brood patch is obvious when the bird is in the hand.

five years in succession and during that period successfully reared four broods of four young. The only failure was in 1982 when the nest was washed out at the clutch stage in a spell of incessant rain.

The majority of birds caught are hens which is natural as they spend much more of their time in the vicinity of the nest than the cock birds. Other than the Stables the only territory where a hen nested for more than two years in succession was at the Dam which had the same bird for three seasons. In the same territory there were four different hens in five years. Typical of the kestrel's unpredictability, as patterns were beginning to develop, the sequences at both the Limekilns and the Dam were broken when hens missed a year then came back to nest again in the same sites. The reasons for this behaviour can only be conjecture though these birds certainly did not breed in nearby sites on their sabbatical year. Two hens have, however, been caught in two territories in different years. One bred in Waterhead and was caught the next year in the Magpie Wood which is less than a kilometre away. However there is no evidence that a failed breeding attempt one year causes a hen to move away to another territory the following season. (Adult changeover details are illustrated in Table 1).

Table 1   The adult changeover (hens) in selected territories

	1980	1981	1982	1983	1984	1985	1986	1987	1988	1989	1990
Dam	A	A	A	B	NB	C	D	C	C	D	E
Coastal Cliff	NB	NB	A	A	B	B	NB	C	C	NB	NB
Limekilns	NC	NC	NC	NC	A	B	A	C	D	E	F
Kenbain	NC	NC	NC	A	B	B	C	D	D	NB	NB
Lowland Quarry	NC	NC	A	B	NB	NB	C	D	E	D	F
Gable End	NC	NC	A	B	NB	C	NC	D	E	F	G

key	Each different letter on each line represents a different hen
	NB pair did not breed in that year
	NC hen was not caught

Although there is definite evidence that adult birds usually return to the same locality to breed in successive years, no bird ringed as a chick has been caught as a breeding adult in its natal territory. One chick, ringed two territories to the north, was found breeding three years later on the Coastal Cliff. At the other end of the spectrum, Andy Village caught one of the birds I'd ringed as a youngster breeding in one of his sample territories in Eskdalemuir.

What is most encouraging is that no breeding attempt has been adversely affected by birds being trapped. The cock bird is more elusive, but on several occasions in warm weather time has been taken to trap the pair in the knowledge that the eggs would not be chilled. The only cock bird which was caught regularly was a very bold individual at the Gable End territory. He bred successfully for three years with two different hens, each time using a different nest site. Work in Holland has shown that ringed adults are often present in the same locality in successive breeding seasons but not necessarily at the same site.

There is clearly much more long-term work needed before generalisations can be confidently made but I suspect that the quick turnover of adults fits in with the kestrels overall breeding strategy – a high reproductive rate of young fledging to compensate for a relatively short adult life.

What is not in doubt is that the trapping in May generates many of the adrenalin-pulsing incidents during a season. The excitement of a retrap is often matched by the actual trapping. On one occasion I climbed down the wire at Kenbain to find the hen still in the nest site and after a brief struggle she was cornered at the back of the cavity. The one-handed climb up the wire was – character building! On another occasion at the Gable End I had not taken the trap in with me and could see the hen sitting in the hole. The prospect of a long haul back to the car did not appeal so I took off my jacket, slipped two pieces of wood which were conveniently at hand up the arms, and spent ten painstaking minutes

The author about to release the hen kestrel at the Gable End after ringing.

crawling to a position below the nest hole. The jacket was thrown up over the entrance and the bird obligingly flew into it and was caught. I have never seen Duncan so impressed.

The year 1990 even surpassed this impressive catch. Armed with a net, I had crawled in through bone-dry vegetation until I was in the strike position below the nest hole. After a reasonable rest to calm the tenseness caused by the approach, I clamped the net over the entrance. She came out like a rocket into the fine mesh but incredibly the head came off the handle and the net fell back. Momentarily held she regained her composure and launched herself into the air. Instinctively, I dived and grabbed for her and miraculously caught her with both hands. There I was lying on my back, arms held high, grasping a bewildered kestrel. Duncan's comments cannot be repeated here! In both these instances I would make the point that the birds were totally unharmed and went on to rear their young. The first incident is certainly a blemish on an otherwise clean record, the second was sheer instinct.

The condition of the adults varies considerably from individual to individual. The heaviest hen caught was 332 g, a fine specimen which nested at the Dam in 1984 and succeeded in a clean sweep – laid six eggs, hatched six young and reared them all. Ironically the lightest hen caught was also recorded at the Dam, weighing a paltry 235 g, and, although she laid a good clutch of five eggs, none hatched. Some of the hens are well into the moult by the middle of May and can have several feathers missing while others are simply in poor condition. This can happen if they are cooped up on a ledge, or in a box or hole for long periods during incubation, especially during inclement weather. One hen at the Gable End

Gable End hen showing the poor condition of the tail feathers prior to moulting.

KESTREL FEATHER MOULT

The moulting of old feathers which have become less efficient due to wear and tear is a vital part of any bird's annual cycle. Feathers are vital for flight, waterproofing, display, temperature control and camouflage and are maintained assiduously by preening, using the bill. This rearranges the feathers, relocates the tiny barbs on the vane of the feather, removes lice and lubricates the feathers with oil.

In the kestrel, the moult strategy is a feather by feather replacement, the old feathers gradually being pushed out by the new which grow up from below. The spread-out time scale of the moult ensures that the bird is never impaired to the extent that it cannot fulfil its role in the breeding cycle. The largest feathers are the 10 primaries and 13 secondaries on the wing and the 12 tail feathers. The hen kestrel starts her wing moult during incubation from late April to mid May and finishes in early September. The discarded moult feathers often give a clue to the location of a nest site. The cock bird starts two weeks later but apparently finishes at about the same time.

The sequence of the moult on the wing starts with Primary 4 and progresses towards the body (ascendantly) and away from the body (descendently) giving the following pattern. There is some individual variation:

4   5   6   7   (8 or 2)   9   1   10

The secondaries are moulted at the same time, ascendantly and descendently from feather 5. The upper wing coverts begin to moult after two weeks, the main tail feathers after 21 – 23 days and the under wing coverts after 50 days. The wing moult takes approximately 130 days, while the body moult is much more protracted, lasting most of the year.

Juveniles begin to moult soon after they have fledged. They undergo a slow, partial moult of the body from autumn to the following summer. Some retain their juvenile feathers until August of their second year. The juvenile wing and tail replacement takes place from June/July to October/November of their second year. Some juvenile kestrels which breed in their first year do so in pre-adult plumage.

had a tail with every one of the 12 feathers having a broken ragged tip.

Occasionally a bird will show signs of a past injury especially on the legs which come in for real pressure as they are constantly hitting the ground when prey is taken. Missing claws are an occupational hazard. One of the most unusual sights was a tick clinging tenaciously to the eyelid of a Limekilns' hen. No attempt was made to remove the offending parasite which must have caused the bird considerable irritation as it sated itself on the unfortunate kestrel's blood. Once more the eventual outcome of the breeding attempt was unaffected and five young were fledged.

To give a flavour of the fieldwork at this time and the ups and downs which characterise catching I can do no better than recall a day in early June 1986.

Diary extract – On Safari with Smith, 6 June:

The tick was clinging tenaciously to the eyelid of the Limekilns hen.

An outing with Don Smith to do the rounds at Darvel.

The weather was threatening rain but so far only a few spots had hit the Land Rover windscreen. Hardly a mile up the road, through attractive mixed farmland, and Don's camera was out with an indecently long lens to photograph an oystercatcher on its nest – in the bow of a dead tree above a hedge. Oystercatchers seem to delight in choosing unusual sites as several have used the hollowed out tops of fence posts in Ayrshire recently. Photography out of the way, it was across a fairly wet field and a further march through awkward wind-blown timber with a ladder to the horrendous larch which hopefully housed the kestrels.

The hen kestrel dutifully came off the old crow's nest occupied last year by long-eared owls. Situated 15 metres above the ground the climb to the nest did pose real difficulties as the branches began at 8 metres and the ladder was woefully short. A touch of apprehension as I climbed the rungs was well justified as the stretch to the first possible bough had no hand holds. It was a case of arms and legs wrapped round the trunk and a painful slow haul up to the elusive branch.

By the time my feet were on the branch and the heavy breathing had reduced to mere gasps, the shakes had set in. Two minutes' rest despite Don's uncomplimentary remarks coming from the safety of terra firma. Straight-forward now and the confirmation of a clutch of four eggs. As nests go it was on its last legs. Young crows one year, then young long-eared owls the next had taken their toll and it wouldn't last another season. Indeed it possibly wouldn't hold out for the next few weeks as the cup was paper thin and you could see through the matrix of sticks.

The descent was no easier and both arms and stomach were badly bruised! Larch are probably the least trustworthy of trees to climb. The trap set, we moved off to a vantage point but although she came in she didn't settle. Frustrated we abandoned the attempt and removed the trap. The bird's welfare always comes first.

Compounding our despondency, the Land Rover stuck in the field — not an uncommon occurrence over the years with Don. I can still remember the day I was nearly catapulted from the vehicle on one narrow muddy track at the Stables which was our next port of call. The birds had been seen in the old ruined stables on a previous visit so we parked nearby and walked in silently to check. Clapping did nothing so we resorted to the ladder again as the rain began to patter on the surrounding leaves. The kestrels had previously nested in a variety of holes near the top of the walls which had supported rafters in the past. Three holes were checked and the spectre of another blank loomed. Up the ladder for the last time and no sooner had my head come level with the hole than a hen kestrel scurried back into the recess off five eggs.

The final haul over the nest rim was greeted by two pairs of beautiful orange eyes as the long-eared owlets backed off.

Incredibly she'd sat tight during the less-than-quiet moving of the ladder and probably had done the same on the previous visit. Very slowly I edged my hand in and caught her easily. My delight at the capture was somewhat tempered by the realisation that she was a young bird and unringed, thus bringing an end to the sequence of breeding by the old hen which had used the alternative tree site for five years.

Another diary extract illustrates one of the pleasures of the kestrel work, namely contact with the rest of the wildlife which shares the Ayrshire countryside with my chosen subject.

Diary extract — 15 May 1987:

Weather holding and another session at the Waterhead study area on the cards. The car can almost find its own way there now and, because it was Friday night with no school the next day, my son Keith came along too. Deirdre dropped me off at Waterhead and went to park the car while I checked the box. No bird came off but I wasn't too worried as she often left when the car door banged. The tree was climbed on auto pilot and the six eggs were warm. Trap set, we retired to the vantage point. Keith had spotted the hen circling a few times as we worked and she flew over as we settled down and disappeared into the face of the wood. It was difficult to see what was happening as the setting sun was directly in our eyes and the wood was just a dark profile. However, with shaded binoculars, a light shape was picked out in a tree on the edge of the shelter belt. As our eyes got used to the conditions the immobile outline was recognisable as a bird, but what species?

After ten minutes, when no kestrel appeared on the skyline, Deirdre walked towards the wood while I concentrated on the shape. It scuttled into the dense cover of the sitka branches. Hardly the reaction of a hen kestrel, and when an adult owl left the vicinity of the shape a few minutes later and floated under the canopy into the wood, my guess was that we had a long-eared owl's nest.

The hen had had plenty of time to be caught so we decided to go in. We had her and what a catch. She was huge, in a fierce temper and already ringed. Handling her brought pin pricks of blood to the hands but the number was eventually taken down and she weighed in at an impressive 330 g.

Leaving the wood the 'Owl tree' was checked and the pellets on the ground merited another climb. At first the signs were not good but, after about five metres, the mass of small white droppings indicated success. Another three metres and the shape of the nest appeared. An adult took off and the final haul over the nest rim was greeted with bill snapping and two pairs of beautiful orange eyes. The long-eared owlets were well-developed, probably three weeks old. The smell and the midges were both overpowering and with a final glance of admiration I skimmed down to join the team. Our hefty female kestrel was released well away from the wood and quickly headed back to the nesting area.

92

The sequel to the long-eared owl breeding attempt was quite interesting. On a later visit to the study area, I was checking a small stand of conifers about three-quarters of a kilometre from the owl nest site when I found an owlet. It was the same age as the nestlings at Waterhead but no nest was visible in this copse. The owlet, which was cowering on the ground, was in a filthy state, feathers matted and eyes completely encased with dirt. It could not open its eyes and was light as a feather when picked up. It really had no chance of survival and presumably had been carried from the nest site and been dumped here by adults. Both the distance and nature of the terrain, ploughed forestry ground, completely ruled out the owlet having made the journey itself.

I really had little choice and carried the pathetic bundle of feathers to the car and set off home. It took nearly half an hour to bathe it until the two red eyes were fully operational again. Food was gorged ravenously and within a few days it was a totally different bird. Happily it was hacked back to the nest and presumably flew successfully.

The supporting cast can indeed make a visit to a kestrel territory like the Coastal Cliff even more interesting. In the late sixties and early seventies, the cliff adjacent to the kestrel eyrie supported several pairs of house martins which built their mud domes directly on to the lava face. Unfortunately they have not used the site for at least 15 years. The sea is always capable of turning up a surprise. It's not unusual on a July visit to the site to see large numbers of basking sharks close inshore but even more impressive was a turtle of undetermined species which held us spellbound one day as it laboured down the Clyde. My one and only sighting of this creature in British waters. Synchronised swimming by red-breasted mergansers is also a feature offshore as non-breeding birds fish in parties of up to 20.

Some of the territories have been given names following incidents at the nest site. A small wood among lowland mixed farmland, planted in the past for game bird cover became the Mallard Wood when a duck came off a dozen eggs at the base of the tree in which the kestrel was breeding. Eventually she just sat tight when the tree was climbed and on the occasions when she was off taking a break the clutch was covered with a thick layer of down.

One evening on which Mike Callan and I drew a complete blank with kestrels will never be forgotten because of two nest sites side by side. Imagine a boulder-strewn upland river, reduced to a trickle by a dry spell, on the fringe of upland moor and sitka plantations. Up a bank stood two gnarled old tree stumps just over two metres high. The reaction to peering into the first was a hissing sound and the second a persistent clicking. The hissing came from a duck goosander which refused to be intimidated by our presence. She raised her neck and crest, fanned out her tail and defied us to come any closer. Not once did she expose her clutch of eggs, nesting on a bed of white down, despite her fury. Photography was not easy but, with the aid of a torch, I was able to focus on her head one metre down in the depths. The sequel to the breeding attempt was Mike and his father having to rescue three of the ducklings, which had not managed to escape from the very deep nest cavity, and reunite them with the family far downstream.

The duck goosander refused to be intimidated and posed for photographers.

Next door, in stump number two, was a tawny owl fast asleep beside two owlets whose bills clicked so much that the adult was rudely awakened. Seeing that the exit was blocked she just lay still and played possum. Not so the owlets which surged up the inside of the trunk at an alarming speed and required restraining. Finally they too settled down and were photographed. Just to finish off the evening we found an oystercatcher on three eggs on the boulder scree and another in the top of a gate post further downstream. It's at moments like this that you realise that the kestrel is just one component of the intricate web of wildlife on the hill.

YOUNG IN THE NEST

Calculations made at the time when the first eggs were found enable me to target each nest site very accurately to record the next vital piece in the jigsaw — the hatching data. Most kestrel pairs do not lay their first egg till the middle of April in Ayrshire, except in exceptional years, so it's mid-May before the chicks begin to break out of their protective shells.

If possible, when a hatch is imminent or has just occurred, I give plenty of warning of my approach otherwise the young can be inadvertently carried out of the nest by the panic exit of the brooding bird. Even during the course of normal activities, such as the hen coming off the nest to receive food from the cock bird, the vulnerable newly hatched chicks can be dragged out of the protective bowl of the nest scrape. On several occasions, at the Limekilns and Kenbain for example, the hens have retrieved their displaced offspring but only if they are relatively close to the rim. One unfortunate youngster at Kenbain fell through the sticks of the old raven's nest and although an initial attempt was made by the hen to search for it, she didn't persevere long and presumably the tiny chick perished.

The chicks can be heard tapping and feebly cheeping inside the eggs even before they begin the process of chipping their way out, about 24−28 hours before hatching. They emerge with the help of the egg tooth, a small, hard, triangular projection on the upper mandible, which is used to great effect in making the first break in the shell. The small hole is gradually enlarged in linear fashion, round the central area of the egg, until the eggshell breaks into two. Sometimes this is not a clean cut and the shell just breaks up.

The hen will assist the young out of the egg and will remove the shells from the nest, often just throwing them over the rim. Otherwise they just allow them to be trampled into fragments and become part of the nest debris. The chicks emerge wet and exhausted, barely able to raise their heads and with their eyes closed. They are tiny, weighing only 15−21 g, less than a small tube of mints.

In most cases the hatching is asynchronous, and a clutch of five eggs normally takes 3−5 days before all the chicks are out. Only in two cases have I found all the eggs hatching on the same day. One was in a nest high in a sitka

An egg showing the first incision made by the emerging chick with its egg tooth.

spruce, where one chick was just out of the egg, and all the rest were at various stages of emerging.

An interesting phenomenon is the hiding of food at this crucial period in the cycle. One crow's nest was literally bulging with decapitated voles. Seven were laid round the perimeter of the nest in readiness for the chicks. In another cliff site I found four voles tucked into vegetation at the cock bird's favourite perch. This would have obvious advantages if the weather was inclement and inhibited hunting just after the young had hatched.

Although the hatching rate is very high (nearly three-quarters of eggs laid hatch and almost half the clutches hatch completely) bizarre accidents can happen at this time. Some eggs do not hatch because they have been chilled at some point during incubation when the hen has been kept off for one reason or another, and the chicks are dead in the shell. Other eggs may be infertile. One young kestrel had the good fortune to be rescued on one of the scheduled visits. All but one of the eggs in this particular batch had hatched but, by a freak chance, one of the discarded shells had been jammed on to the end of the last egg and had stuck like glue when it dried. The weak cries from within shattered all vestiges of objectivity and I carefully prised off the offending shell and assisted the bedraggled waif out into the wide world.

Another incident happened at the Quiet Glen, a place I never tire of. The long drive is always full of promise as the road meanders alongside the upper reaches of a boulder-stream river where dipper and goosander feed. My last sighting of a corncrake in Ayrshire was of a bird taking off from a grassy verge, caught in the headlights as I travelled home at dusk. It was a bird on passage in early spring, heading possibly for its last stronghold in the Western Highlands and Islands. When I first came to Ayrshire you could drive up some of the lowland valleys in the late evening and list up to 10 or 12 of these birds in monotonous vocal competition. Alas they are a rare sight now, having declined dramatically nationwide, due to pressure on their grassland niche through drainage. Cropping for silage was the death knell as adults, clutches and broods were inadvertently mown by the machinery before the breeding cycle could be completed. However I digress.

The regiments of sitka which now engulf the Glen are well managed for wildlife thanks to the Manager, John Wykes, and enough grassland has been left unplanted in the forest strategy to support one pair of kestrels, though the barn owl has sadly departed. A stand of mature sitka, numbering about 40 trees, stuck out like a beacon among the young trees. I must have climbed most of them in pursuit of the kestrel. The small wood is also home for a pair of sparrowhawks, tawny owls which insist on using the kestrel nest box and, thankfully, a pair of carrion crows whose architectural skills are utilised by the kestrels.

A few years ago the resident kestrel pair used a very exposed crow platform in the top-most whorl of branches in a majestic sitka spruce. Despite the open nature of the site, the hen laid a full clutch of five eggs and at the appropriate date I crossed the river and climbed the tree. She came off the nest when I was half-

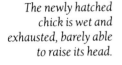

The newly hatched chick is wet and exhausted, barely able to raise its head.

way up but the euphoria evaporated when I found four warm but dead chicks and an unhatched egg in the nest bowl. The young were all the same age, no more than two days old. They had not hatched together as two were beginning to decompose in the head and one could not have been more than a few hours dead. All were slightly flattened which was possibly the clue to their demise. Being so exposed and under regular harassment from the crows which nested nearby I concluded that her inexperience had led to her flattening herself on to the nest to protect the young, causing them to suffocate. She had been caught a few weeks earlier and was certainly a first year bird.

There's no doubt that the time of hatching is the second real pressure point in the cycle. Following the relatively easy incubation spell the pair move into a much more demanding phase. The cock bird especially has to accelerate food production from the equivalent of four voles per day to as many as 28. He does not usually become involved with the hatching, the hen being very protective at this time as I witnessed at one site when the cock bird nearly came to grief when he ventured too close. The hen had left the nest when I had been walked into the hide on the quarry top. He just happened to arrive back with food just after I settled in. Getting no response from the hen he flew into the nest site which contained four newly hatched chicks. No sooner had he landed by the nest than a brown blur shot over the quarry rim and knocked him off the ledge. Luckily he recovered his composure before hitting the quarry floor and left the area in a hurry. This is also the time when the hen will take liberties with humans and I've several times been buffeted while inspecting a nest.

True to form with the kestrel there was one exception to the rule. I was ensconced in the hide at the Dam looking through the lens at three newly hatched chicks and two unhatched eggs when the calls of an approaching bird put me in a state of readiness. Much to my surprise the cock bird landed on the ledge and ran into the nest. He stood there, unsure, a newly killed vole dangling from his beak. His initial hesitation soon subsided and he stepped forward, placed the vole at his feet and began to tear small pieces of vole from the carcase. The chicks' response to his proffered titbits was absolutely nil as they lay, heads resting on the eggs.

PROFILE OF THE SHORT-TAILED FIELD VOLE

The short-tailed field vole (*Microtus agrestis*) is undoubtedly the favoured prey item of the kestrel. Research work has shown that peaks in the number of kestrel young ringed coincides with years when voles are particularly abundant. Voles do fluctuate markedly on a local scale with peaks occurring every four to five years. This general agreement between high vole numbers and ringing is illustrated in the north of England and Scotland with peaks in 1926, 1933, 1938, 1944, 1948 & 49, 1952, 1957, 1961 and 1964.

The food requirement of the kestrel is about one-fifth of its body weight per day (36−68 g) or the equivalent of two average-sized voles. The claim made in the late Seton Gordon's book *Hill Birds of Scotland* may be a slight exaggeration:

> . . . that a single kestrel, remaining in a district for 210 days will be the means of destroying no less than 10,395 mice.

The field vole is small, greyish-brown and easily recognised by its blunt snout and short tail. In Britain this small mammal inhabits mainly rough ungrazed grassland including forestry plantations at the early stage of development when the growth of lush grass provides good feeding and cover. In years of vole abundance the upland pasture is often crisscrossed by well-formed runways and pock-marked with burrow entrance holes. Well-used tunnels are characterised by small heaps of cut grass stems and green droppings.

Four to six young are produced in each of a series of litters from spring to late autumn coinciding with the breeding season of the kestrel, and individuals born at the early part of the season usually reproduce in the same year. The young are born in nests constructed often at the base of grass tussocks and are weaned between two and four weeks later. Females become sexually mature in as short a time as three weeks and may mate in six weeks. The potential for a rapid increase of the population is great.

Microtus agrestis is active throughout 24 hours a day and this accounts for the fact that their characteristic yellow incisors are so often found in the pellets of not only kestrels, but buzzards, barn owls, tawny owls, long- and short-eared owls, harriers and even herons. It also falls prey to mammalian predators like the fox, stoat, weasel, polecat and pine marten.

The short-tailed field vole is the preferred prey of the kestrel.

THE VOLE PLAGUES OF 1890

Remarkably, in the face of all the persecution during the Victorian period, the kestrel entered the twentieth century on a high note — courtesy of the plagues of voles in the Scottish Borders. The cyclic nature of vole population dynamics in upland areas often features regular peaks which can result in sheep pasture being cropped by large numbers of these small mammals.

A particularly spectacular plague occurred in 1890 in the counties of Roxburgh, Dumfries, Lanark and Kirkcudbright. Such had been the concern expressed by the farmers and the accusations raised that the plague was caused by the eradication of vermin, that advice had been sought from skilled naturalists. Their recommendation was that the natural enemies of the voles should be encouraged.

Even the gamekeepers, who had succeeded in ridding most of the hill area of 'vermin', co-operated with an early moratorium on the killing of birds of prey and the result was a natural response from kestrels and short-eared owls in this time of plenty. The numbers of avian predators was such that they received much praise in the local press for their sterling work in dealing with the vole problem.

Peter Adair, in a survey published in 1892, collected comments and figures from farmers in the areas where the damage was greatest. Four examples of the comments are as follows:

'In the Devils Beef Tub alone there were 18 nests.'
'Very numerous. 30 seen together.'
'Great numbers — 6 nests in an old crow wood.'
'8–10 pairs on the farm.'

It must have been an incredibly productive time for the kestrel and short-eared owl and Adair's estimate of the latter species in one season was 602 nests and over 4,000 reared! He concludes his paper by stating that in the vole-infested area the kestrel was constantly in sight, sometimes several at once and that they formed a most pleasing feature of the landscape.

Another commentator of the time, Richard Bell of Castle O'er in the same area, recalled a previous vole plague in 1876–77 which, though not as severe, had attracted large numbers of short-eared owls and rough-legged buzzards. More importantly Bell, who farmed at Crurie as well as Castle O'er, gives an indication of the rich raptor population of the area:

I did not employ a gamekeeper, and consequently my 'vermin' went unmolested, and in my woods were bred annually a great number of owls — of the two species, the Barn and the Long-eared — as well as many Sparrowhawks and Kestrels. These last, in the absence of more congenial nesting places, built in the fir trees . . . when the plague broke out these birds forsake my woods and went to the 'moused ground'.

An early and clear example of predators responding to prey populations rather than the reverse.

Much to my surprise the cock kestrel at the Dam site landed and moved into the nest.

Undeterred by the lack of response from the chicks he proceeded to settle down and brood.

Undeterred by their negative response he pushed the vole to the back of the nest and boldly stood over the young. Shuffling his feathers he settled down on the brood, tail leaning against the wall. His nest duty lasted half an hour until the hen's calls alerted him and he left at speed to allow her to resume the normal pattern. This was not an isolated incident as he was twice more filmed brooding in the first week of young in the nest.

On one other occasion, at the Ram Wood, the cock bird put in an appearance. I quote from the diary.

Diary extract – 24 May 1987:

What a relief to taste the solitude of the hill after a torrid day in the Park. A holiday weekend and sunshine equals approximately 3,500 people, and today was no exception. We set off for the Ram Wood, laden like packhorses, with the intention of completing the hide and catching the hen. Wooden ribs for the hide, the bucket and foam cushion for seating, brace and bits for drilling holes, a saw, trap and camera gear were all carefully shared out. The ground was drying nicely but we still had to leap over long-unattended ditches now almost level with deceptive sphagnum moss. A spotted flycatcher flew along the edge of the wood but nothing else stirred.

Even when we'd dumped the gear under the hide tree, the bird didn't leave the box, and it was only when I was half-way up with the first load that she condescended to depart.

Immediately, the sound of young chicks was heard and, sure enough, when I drew level with the box the middle of the scrape was just a white jumble of down. It was difficult to assess how many chicks had hatched but at least four beaks were counted at one time. Egg shells had been discarded at the side and what looked like prey items lay at the back. The whole complexion of the evening changed.

Working as quickly as possible, nine metres above ground level, the holes were drilled, the sticks inserted and the hide took shape. The kestrel hen had obviously accepted the green material so it was worth an attempt to do a reconnaissance for photography later on in the week. Deirdre ferried the material up while I worked on the platform, and twenty minutes later I was couched reasonably comfortably behind the camera gear while Keith and Deirdre left to check Waterhead and the Magpie Wood.

The chicks were making subdued calls and within five minutes the chaffinch and mistle thrush alarm sounded the adult's return. The distinctive clip call was heard from a few trees away, then he landed on the branch a few metres away from the box. He was immaculate, his feather condition superb and a shaft of the low evening sun caught his blue nape, tail and rufus back. Without any hesitation he ran along the branch, perched briefly on the rim of the box, and moved in. He circled the chicks which responded with heads raised and more muted cries but he just ruffled his feathers and settled down to brood.

The quiet domestic scene didn't last long as the hen came back calling

Healthy brood after a week.

loudly. He responded immediately by leaving the box. She landed on the branch with a fat, decapitated vole in her beak and moved directly into the box. Again, positioned at the back, she firmly held the food in her talons and began to tear tiny fragments of meat and proffer them very delicately to the open beaks, slightly inclining her head as she did so. The chicks were not really interested and after a couple of abortive attempts she laid the vole to the side and, like the cock bird, ruffled her feathers and settled down. It took her two or three minutes to tuck all the young under her feathers, gently manipulating them with her beak. The chicks were obviously new born and she treated them with infinite care. She'd laid her first egg on 18 April so, true to form, she must have begun incubating after the third egg. She was now completely relaxed and apart from a few minor adjustments just sat looking out of the box.

When Deirdre and Keith arrived back after an hour, the hen kestrel slipped off and we packed up quickly. The gear was brought down in a couple of minutes. A quick shin up the nest tree confirmed a complete hatch of six and that a cache of prey was tucked in at the back — pieces of vole and two untouched shrews.

The first seven days are probably the most vulnerable time for the family. The young are helpless, unable to stand, covered in a thin white down and in need of almost constant brooding and attention from the hen. She rarely leaves the confines of the nest site except to pick up food from the cock bird. He usually calls her to him and rarely ventures into the site himself. She brings the food back, inevitably decapitated and, holding it down with her feet, tears off small pieces of

The young look like tiny vultures, supporting themselves on their pot bellies.

Even at an early age the chicks will cough up pellets.

red meat. She offers it gently to the young which are soon satisfied and slump back into the prone position. She then finishes off the remainder of the food. The food is passed bill to bill.

Even at this stage, the young birds deposit droppings over the nest,'but for the most part they lie and sleep in the nest scrape. If they do raise themselves up they do so on their elbows supporting themselves on their obscene pot bellies. I always imagine them as tiny vultures at this time. Their claws are soft and harmless and the egg tooth, which assisted their emergence into the world, is still visible after five days.

If young are lost due to natural causes this normally takes place in the first week and it is invariably the last-hatched chick which dies. They are occasionally squashed, especially if the site is small and cramped and movement restricted. If food is scarce the youngest is usually the first to succumb being unable to compete with the older and stronger siblings.

The resilience of the newly hatched chicks was amply illustrated by one remarkable incident at Kenbain in 1987. On a routine check at the site the hen was seen coming off at a changeover and a white bundle of fluff was carried over the nest rim and tumbled down the cliff into the long grass below. A quick dash up to the base of the cliff and a frantic search by Keith and I eventually recovered the tiny, newly hatched chick which was still breathing. Nothing ventured, nothing gained; I climbed up the cliff and edged my way along the ledge until I was within striking distance of the crow's nest. The gap of two metres was impossible to

The hen kestrel gently proffers a piece of meat to the well-disciplined chick.

negotiate so, heart in mouth, I took aim and lobbed the chick through the air. It landed, thankfully, bang on top of its nest mates and lay still. Not giving a lot for its chances we left, planning a visit in a few days' time to confirm the outcome. Not only did the chick survive its second 'flight', it thrived and was ringed three weeks later. Truly a survivor.

After the first week the chicks develop a second, thicker and heavier down layer. This is buff-grey above and paler below. The hen still attends to her nest duties and feeds the chicks but small items of prey are eaten whole (with great effort) by the end of the second week. One eleven-day-old chick took a full six minutes to swallow a shrew which it had grabbed from the hen as soon as she alighted on the nest. The shrew went in head first and at one point I thought the bird was about to choke. It persevered and eventually, after much pumping of the neck, the last piece of black fur disappeared. The chick then slept it off, taking no part in the next three feeding sessions.

The hen still protects the young from the elements, mantling to shield them from excessive sun and rain. She is usually an excellent parent and will retrieve any wanderers. One very lucky youngster which had crawled out of the nest was plucked at the last second from the rim of the quarry and dangling in the hen's beak was carried back to the safety of the brood. Two-week-old chicks still lie in the nest bowl and, except in very dry locations, their underparts tend to become very dirty. The underside of the legs, which are continually stretched out under the body become smooth and devoid of feathers. Towards the end of the second week the hen begins to spend less and less time at the actual nest site but still remains in close attendance.

A brood in the second week, the white down being replaced by buff-grey.

One special moment at the hatching period will always stay with me and is probably the high point of the whole kestrel work to date.

Diary extract — 10 June 1987:

By the time we'd begun the trek to the Limekilns the weather caught up with us and light rain swiftly became driving rain. Just the conditions I needed for a climb! In reality the face of the Limekilns was relatively dry. Unfortunately my boots were not, but I was determined to round off the hatching data by checking the site. Unusually for the Limekilns' kestrels, the pair had laid a late clutch and were well behind the rest of the population. In the end, after a series of slips, Deirdre climbed the back of the building and, supported by a rope, I just managed to ease myself up.

I should have guessed that the hen would be on the nest, but it was still a surprise when I peered in to find her peering out. As I braced myself for the high speed escape (a definite *déjà vu*), she merely retreated, exposing a bundle of tiny, white, newly hatched bodies. Very, very cautiously I stretched my arm in and separated four minute bodies and an unhatched egg.

All the time, no more than five centimetres from my finger tips, she remained stock still, her eyes following every movement. It was a very special moment, being so close to this intimate scene, and it was with great reluctance that I slowly retreated leaving her to resume her duties.

Blank, fruitless evenings are forgotten at such times. The satisfaction was as much in being able to control the situation once it arose and leave the bird and its brood almost as I'd found it, yet having gained the information required.

The author's son, Keith, with a brood at the ideal age for ringing.

RINGS AND ROPES

By the time I began studying the kestrel seriously, several scientific papers had been published which indicated that juvenile kestrels dispersed and migrated, some for long distances. The basis of these statements came from the analysis of kestrel ringing recoveries from the British Trust for Ornithology's ringing scheme. However, little was known about the dispersal of young kestrels from Ayrshire until the regular ringing of broods began from 1975 onwards. There were always plenty of birds about all year round in Ayrshire, but were they locals?

The main thrust of the work in June is to ring the various broods with a view to building up a picture of what happens when the young birds leave the nest. By the end of the 1990 season, I had ringed 980 nestlings from 238 broods, of which a grand total of 65 individuals had been recovered. The totals for each year usually reflected the productivity of the species in that year as I tried to keep the level of fieldwork effort reasonably consistent. The worst year was 1986 when only ten nestlings were ringed, but 1990 more than made up for that when a record 106 was achieved.

The ringing phase is physically demanding as so much time is spent on a rock face, or high in a sitka spruce, collecting the chicks, and carefully placing them in cloth bags before carrying them down to ground level to be processed. Very often the easiest way to descend is to grip the draw strings of the bags in your teeth, thus reducing the chance of their being crushed. In extremely hazardous situations the easiest way to transport the chicks is by putting them down your sweater, always making sure that it (the sweater) is tucked in! Once on the ground, the individuals are weighed, ringed, measured and invariably photographed before they are returned to the nest.

The adults' reaction to human intruders at this time varies, but the alarm calls of the chicks very often spurs individuals into action. At the Ram Wood one year a pair used a crow's nest at the very top of an imposing spruce. While I collected the young for ringing, the pair kept up a barrage of calling and came within two or three metres of the nest while I was precariously perched in a very exposed spot. The norm however is to register disapproval at a safe distance.

Timing is fairly crucial. A wasted evening can be a setback when timetabling is tight, so visiting a nest when the young are at an optimum size for ringing is vital. If they are too small, there is the possibility that the aluminium ring may slip over the claws and cause injury or disfigurement. If they are too old, handling can be difficult and painful as they can not only scatter from the nest but also defend themselves quite well by raking intruders with their talons. That is the last thing you need 15 metres up a swaying tree. The ideal age to ring the chicks is at 14 days, when they tend to be placid and large enough to keep a ring on.

However, when in the field, circumstances often dictate ringing on the spot. The Crumbling Quarry is very well named and one climb per season is enough for the nerves. It is a large hill quarry, surrounded by open grassland, ideal kestrel hunting grounds. Unfortunately, the rock faces are fragmented and completely unstable making climbing or abseiling unpleasant and risky. An extract from the diary describes one ringing session:

Diary extract – 24 June 1986:

Drizzle was the very thing I didn't need for this quarry site. The site had been located by John and Jean Burton but the exact clutch size was not known, as a boulder obscured the full nest. As we approached, the hen left what was now a conspicuously, white-washed ledge and circled the perimeter of the quarry. A pair of whitish wings stretched above the rocks confirming at least one young bird's presence. John threw the support rope down – to an accompanying shower of debris and a hard hat was donned. It was probably the most demanding climb I've attempted even with the help of a rope. Rocks flaked off continually, the helmet was peppered from above, and hand holds were tenuous to say the least. Most of the rock sloped down towards me adding to the degree of difficulty.

Ten minutes' climbing for only six metres and knees were wobbling badly. At no stage was there a stable enough point to rest comfortably but the prize was there, three very fit-looking chicks, backs to the wall and talons at the ready. A single unhatched egg lay in the nest cup. Even at the ledge, the quarry face didn't relent and the ringing was done only by supporting my weight on an elbow wedged into the nest ledge and toe ends precariously balanced in cracks. No time was wasted in ringing the trio but not before blood was spilt – all mine. The young were just beginning to show their first quills and by the amount of pipit feathers scattered round the nest the kestrel pair were feeding inland on the higher ground.

The descent was even worse and, but for the supporting rope, it would have been almost impossible. It took another ten minutes to reach the base and the same again to recover. There must be easier ways to spend your leisure time.

At the beginning of the third week, the first feathers begin to appear on the wings and tails of the young and activity in the nest increases. Pestered incessantly while at the nest the hen confines her visits to feeding times, but she will come in

BIRDS IN THE DIET

Birds are a very important secondary source of prey especially during winter, in the June/July period and in urban locations. In hard weather during the winter, when small mammals are difficult to locate, small birds offer an important alternative and in the later stages of the kestrel breeding cycle birds form a vital bulk item in the diet. Inexperienced young meadow pipits, skylarks and starlings are the most vulnerable species in upland territories, while in urban areas the ubiquitous house sparrow is top of the list. Young feral pigeons are also taken regularly.

More than fifty species of birds are listed as being taken by kestrels, some quite large and well outside the prey normally taken. These include waders, ducks, gulls, godwits and usually refer to juveniles or nestlings. Kestrels do tackle birds larger than themselves and have been seen devouring adult wood pigeons and hooded crows and also attacking a green woodpecker.

Kestrels will return time and time again to good feeding areas and a fair toll can be exacted on a particular population of birds. Thirty-five kestrel pellets from one district of the New Forest yielded seven blue tit rings, and in Suffolk, after an analysis of local kestrel pellets, no less than eleven bearded tit rings were found.

One of the most impressive and interesting findings was on Bardsey Island (Gwynedd) where, out of three hundred pellets from the roost of a cock kestrel, the warden, Peter Roberts, extracted a massive total of 131 bird rings. The bird's prey included 49 wrens, 46 goldcrests, 20 robins, dunnocks, chiffchaffs, chaffinches, a meadow pipit, rock pipit and a skylark. This bird had obviously found a profitable niche feeding on both the resident passerines and large falls of migrants.

Ornithologists working with rare species must have their objectivity tested to the full when a kestrel proceeds to plunder the young of the species they are studying. This happened to Norman Atkinson in 1974, when many less-than-common little tern chicks were lifted from nests as the local kestrel pair made up to four visits daily to the colony for easy pickings. Further damage was done to other chicks which were found bleeding but still alive near nests, presumably having been dropped as the kestrels were mobbed by irate parents. Russell Nisbit, at Aberlady Bay, had the same experience, losing eight chicks during the 1975 season; and there is a report of another kestrel taking yet more little tern chicks in Towyn.

This trait of returning to an easy prey location can get kestrels into trouble with game rearers as pheasant poults are easy prey at the early stages in their lives if rearing pens are left open-topped. In my 18 years checking nest sites and dissecting pellets I have only found the remains of one pheasant and one grouse chick at the nest or on a plucking post. They very quickly out-grow the preferred prey size for the kestrel.

Kestrels are also regular attenders at bird roosts at dusk but the British 'Top Gun' award must go to the bird which caught a swift at Chichester Cathedral.

Ram Wood:
after two weeks the
cock bird will come
into the nest
to drop off food.

to mantle the brood during inclement weather. The cock bird now comes in and helps to feed but by about 20 days the chicks are capable of tearing prey and feeding themselves. They respond very quickly to the adult alarm calls by crouching in the nest and remain motionless until the danger is past.

The best time for nest site photography is now past. Around the time of hatching and for the first two weeks the hen is very vigilant and nest-bound, the cock bird making occasional visits. By the third week, the cock bird has increased the amount of time spent hunting to cope with the needs of the family food requirements and he is in and out of the nest site very quickly wasting no time. Still, the only way to gain an insight into the family life of the kestrel is to commit the time and effort for hide work. There is no cutting corners. Long sessions cramped in a stifling hide with the birds oblivious to your presence is the only way to observe and record accurately the birds' behaviour at the nest. In tree hides during windy weather *mal de mer* can be an additional hazard and in hot weather the same effect can be horrendous.

Here is a typical extract from a four-hour session at the Ram Wood hide in 1987.

Diary extract – 13 June 1987:

At last the sunshine has penetrated the hills so the family walked me into the hide. The worst part is humping the gear up to the platform, but there was a sting in the tail this time. Tripod in position with camera; young birds present in the nest box; light sufficient for photography – perfect. It was just a case of zipping up the front of the hide and settling down on the foam pad which made the 'Oor Wullie' pail more comfortable. As my backside hit the foam, the rain of the last week was forced out, down and unfortunately up, leaving me to endure the next four hours with a well-lubricated rear end.

Rosie and the children left, chortling, and I settled down to concentrate on film speeds and focusing. The domestic scene was far from clear. Piled in a heap on one side of the box it was impossible to gauge the number of young kestrels, but from the mess at the entrance and the pellet debris, which was now well above the level of the rim, all seemed to be going well. The time was 1540 hrs.

Once the disturbance caused by my entrance passed, the young emerged cautiously from the heap, or at least two did. They now had the characteristic down-covered heads, like barristers' wigs, while the rest of the body was unevenly covered with down and emerging feathers. The tails were now about eight centimetres long. One chick lost no time in reversing to the edge, cocking its tail and firing yet more white-wash on to the spruce branches below. Feeling much more energetic after that, it progressed to an aerobics session, bowing the front of its body and vigorously flapping its sprouting wings, much to the discomfort of its peers. Wing exercise in the confines of the nest box is definitely anti-social behaviour.

Things settled down again with two standing quietly as the rest lay with eyes closed. Maximum head count so far was five, but the sixth could easily still be present. No body had been spotted under the tree. Flies swarmed round the box, drawn in by the odour of decaying prey remains and droppings, and they were watched carefully by the inmates. Chaffinch calls dominated the woodland sound and it was time to listen intently to get an early warning of an adult coming in. The motion of the trees was causing me some discomfort — but after half an hour the body had adjusted to it.

First indication of action was the sharp clip call of the hen at the edge of the wood and possibly a second bird, but it was difficult to tell. Suddenly she was on the branch, a small vole dangling from her beak. Before I could

Feathers appear and the down begins to moult leaving the young with comical lawyers' wigs.

fire the shutter she scuttled along the branch, shot into the box, deposited the prey and without a second glance, turned and departed. Two frames were taken.

Even the young had been caught unawares, but one of the standing birds grabbed the vole in its talons and, although it mantled, wings drooped over the prey and head down, it made no attempt to eat. Instead it continually stamped on it, practising the act of killing which would be so important in the months ahead. Tiring of this after a few minutes, it left the vole and took up its former position. None of the others bothered to move towards the discarded food, an indication of a time of plenty.

Little happened in the next hour. Occasionally one bird would rise and preen, stretch a wing and pad round the box. One thing I had noticed was that little noise had come from the young when the hen came in. I had expected a barage of noise, but it had been a very muted affair. I was now quite certain that she was in the wood and not out hunting as she'd called a couple of times.

At 1710 hrs, the cock bird flew into the wood and gave his recognition call. She replied but it was the male which hit the branch, another vole hanging from a bloodied beak and, like his mate, ran along the branch and jumped into the box. This time their reaction was swift and the young crowded round calling excitedly. He promptly transferred the vole from beak to talons, an eager chick grabbed the body and promptly mantled it. Bemused, he stood for a few seconds then disappeared as quickly as he'd arrived.

Unlike the previous visit, the aftermath was a bit frantic. Stimulated by its nest mate feeding, a second chick barged against it, succeeded in capturing the vole and mantled it. Dust was flying everywhere and it was a full five minutes before things settled down again.

Meanwhile, above the wood, one or perhaps both of the adult kestrels were engaged in a ferocious aerial battle with a crow. The kestrels yikkered furiously, the crows responded with raucous calls, the mistle thrushes were very upset and chaffinch alarm sounded from all corners of the wood. It was a noisy ten minutes, but the tree tops obscured what must have been an interesting encounter. The wood returned to normal.

At 1800 hrs, the cock bird arrived back in the wood and made a second visit to the box to present a decapitated young meadow pipit. Only one bird responded this time and within minutes only a few feathers remained on the rim. It proved to be the final visit of this session as the next hour was completely devoid of activity. The young slept and I tried desperately to stay awake too. The arrival of the family was a great relief as the tight conditions were beginning to cause cramp. They all had a second good laugh at the watermark on the seat of my trousers.

In the last week or so the nest site becomes a very sordid affair, smelling badly, infested with flies in hot weather, moulted down feathers everywhere. The young, sporting their first feathers which are complete by the fourth week, are much more confident about the nest. They resemble clowns, with down sprouting from their heads, under their chins and on their backs.

They still huddle together to doze, but when food comes in it's everyone for themselves. The food is dropped by either adult, one chick succeeds, mantles and fends off his peers. If there is plenty of room on the site, the young will pester the individual which has the food but, on a tight ledge or crow's nest, safety first prevails and the young settle down quickly. One hen was seen feeding the young at 22 days, but none later.

Excess food is stored at the edge and eaten when the birds are hungry. The hen now assists with the family food budget, but the cock bird still takes on the bulk of such duties. If a hen is lost at this stage the cock bird is capable of rearing the young on his own. By now the killing rate has moved into top gear. I have recorded ten voles coming into a nest in six hours but the most recorded in literature is 28 in one day.

Brood survival is very high and once the young hatch they have an excellent chance of surviving. Accidents can happen, and frenetic activity can dislodge a chick which will inevitably perish under the site. Nest collapses do occur and at one tree site near the Limekilns I climbed up to find one chick clinging precariously to the outer shell of the nest. The central cup had fallen out leaving a hole in the middle. Dead chicks below testified to the resilience and luck of the survivor.

Inclement weather can cause a nest to be washed out and, rarely, young have starved in periods of continual rain when little or no food was brought back to the nest. Loss to other predators is rare too. A couple of young were taken from a low-lying nest by a foraging fox but if man is discounted from the equation the success rate is very high.

Two remarkable instances must be penned at this point. The first was from the study area, the other from Lea McNally in Torridon. A well-known peregrine territory, which supported birds in the depths of the decline in the sixties, has two major rock faces, a kilometre apart. In 1975, when the peregrine pair nested on one, the kestrel occupied the other. A violent storm caused the peregrine nest to be washed out at the clutch stage and, unusually, the hen did not re-lay.

The kestrel had a clutch of four and everything seemed to be progressing satisfactorily until Dick Roxburgh phoned to say that the peregrines were in attendance at the kestrel site and that he thought they were rearing the two kestrel chicks. Sure enough, it was the peregrines which hung in the air and screamed abuse at me when I checked it out. Their agitated behaviour confirmed their attachment to the rock face. The ledge itself was littered with pigeon feathers and both kestrel chicks were looking well. There was no sign of the kestrel adults — had they been killed, or simply driven off?

This is not the first time such a takeover has been recorded. Derek Ratcliffe, in his excellent monograph of the peregrine falcon, documents four other instances, all in Scotland. I ringed the two kestrels just prior to fledging. What a fascinating ringing recovery one of these would make. Alas nothing has materialised. Could a peregrine pair complete their responsibilities by teaching the young kestrels to hunt?

Even the mighty golden eagle has been known to take a kestrel and Lea McNally, who has spent a great part of his life studying this majestic bird in the Scottish Highlands, has recorded plucked remains of a kestrel under an eagle roost. He described in a letter to me the demise of a kestrel chick taken from the nest. I can do no better than let him describe the incident.

While near an eagle eyrie one of the adults came in, gliding, parallel to the cliff and only metres from me. Clutched in one foot was the prey. Hard on the eagle's tail, almost riding on it, came a hen kestrel, tiny in relation to the eagle. She was calling persistently, in very obvious distress, a pathetic-sounding, re-iterated, low-pitched call. To me it was eloquent in its anguish.

Bravely, but uselessly, she did not turn off from her pursuit of the eagle until it had swooped out of its glide to land neatly on the eyrie's ledge. I could not see the small prey item clearly on the eyrie from my point but I am sure it had been a young kestrel, taken from the nest ledge.

A moment of high drama indeed.

The surprise element is always present in work of this kind. In June 1990, I had calculated that the brood of kestrels at another dam were ready for ringing but not having visited the site since before the potential hatching date I was unsure as to the progress of the breeding attempt. As my head topped the ladder, my first glance registered three chicks just at the pleasant stage for ringing. My second reaction was one of sheer excitement as two of the brood were cream coloured with beautiful red eyes.

I realised that the two odd-balls were in fact leucistic, a pale form of albinism in which pigments are lost from feathers but not from the rest of the body. Obviously an uncommon occurrence as I had seen at least 2,000 chicks during my

The two kestrel chicks which were reared to the flying stage by a pair of peregrines.

A leucistic chick at the Dam showing the cream-coloured plumage and red eye.

The normal-coloured chick was the odd one out in the brood.

work and never encountered this before. Among the huge flock of barnacle geese which over-winter at Caerlaverock on the Solway there are one or two leucistic individuals which naturally stand out among their peers.

Both birds seemed quite healthy and responded normally to the ringing. A long photographic session followed, as I attempted to make sure that this phenomenon was well and truly recorded for posterity. The inevitable question was – 'would they survive?' Along with the pair reared by the peregrines this will only be confirmed by a ringing recovery. It was certainly a pleasure to see both leucistics flying – you could hardly miss them! Both adults were caught and showed no variance from normal plumage. One to watch for the future.

A brood's reaction to intruders is very spirited. They throw themselves on to their backs and collectively rake the enemy with flashing claws, retreating to the back of the cliff or edge of the nest. In the struggle they may tumble out of the nest such is the intensity of their defiance. This is a particular hazard which we encounter if an older brood is to be ringed or checked. Extreme care must be taken and pressure situations can easily arise. Take the last ringing outing in 1987.

Diary extract – 14 July 1987:

Ringing does not usually take place as late as this but Duncan Cameron had found a late brood after we'd written off finding kestrels in this territory. Just by coincidence, a young kestrel of the same age needed to be hacked back to the wild. It would be a neat coup if both could be achieved at the same time. The territory in question is nicknamed 'The Slog'. Hectare after hectare of middle-aged sitka, forest rides waist-deep in rank vegetation and no paths.

We were soon soaked by the fine rain (the weatherman had been apologetic, but correct), but worse was to come as we reached the first ranks of conifers. The wind died and the clouds of flies materialised to hang in above our heads. Two roe deer were startled, but such was the height of the grasses that we only saw their heads.

Soaked to the waist we plodded on until after half an hour we finally reached the stand of mature conifers. The nest was high in a bushy-topped Scots pine and the white-wash certainly indicated young kestrels, but at what stage? Certainly there were no birds on the branches so we had a chance.

Reluctant to don the leg irons, we tried to throw the rope over the lower branches six metres up, but after a dozen abortive attempts Duncan was forced to come out of retirement and scale the trunk. Eventually, after a battle of wills, he made it to the first decent footholds and tied off. The flies were appalling and as soon as we settled in the one place the midges homed in.

Another three metres and he was level with five very large kestrels which immediately backed to the rear and on to the branches. Suddenly one of the young took off and flew effortlessly round the stand of pines, closely followed by two learners which floated down. After a quick scamper these were safely caught and bagged. Duncan caught the other two and lowered them down in bags on a long line of cord.

All four were quickly ringed and, with the extra bird that we'd brought in, they were hoisted up to an impatient Duncan who was being eaten alive by midges. The problem of a second wave of exploding kestrels was overcome by the technique of putting each bird over the nest rim from below and laying them on their backs. At no time did Duncan raise his head even level with the nest and all five were safely returned. Duncan thankfully slithered down the rope and we left the area at a great pace, trying to out-strip the insect plague.

To give a flavour of the ringing period I can do no better than recount one unexpected and unsurpassed day during a glorious spell of weather in June 1989.

Diary extract – 19 June 1989:

The day began with a phone call from Duncan Cameron who had avoided the heat of the day by setting out early and by breakfast time he had two territories under his belt. Eight chicks at an ideal age for ringing; an evening foray was arranged. Thus motivated I decided to ring the near-docile brood of four kestrels on the wooded cliff below my office.

Up to this moment the progress of my very local pair had been viewed at a distance from the middle branches of a convenient sycamore tree. Although the old sandstone cliff was on a split level, the section which housed the nesting ledge was a good ten metres down. As it turned out I was able to climb across just below the nest but the traverse, which looked easy from the comfort of a tree, would not have been possible without the assistance of safety lines.

Even in the early morning shade it was a sticky climb, but eventually I was perched reasonably securely on a workable ledge. The crunch came when I put my hand in the small canvas bag attached to my belt. No small pliers. I could not believe my complacency. However the time for personal recriminations is not at the end of a rope and fortuitously I still carried the larger pair of pliers which I'd used in the past for young peregrines and tawny owls.

The second surprise was more pleasant. Gradually working through the brood I came upon body number five, slightly smaller than the other four but surviving well. It must have been masked from view by its nest mates on the previous visits. Despite the large tool the rings were fitted satisfactorily and the retreat was accomplished withour further incident.

After lunch it was off to the Nobel Explosives Site in north Ayrshire, a sprawling commercial complex interspersed with large tracts of grassland, dunes, woodland and open space, ideal for kestrels. Five territories are located within its security boundary and after the initial signing of forms, Eddie Miller took me to a ruined brick building on the periphery where one of the pairs had hatched young – numbers unknown.

A rickety ladder was produced and placed against the inside gable. The kestrels entered through a small hole in the masonry near the top and nested in the depression formed by a few old bags in a small metal frame, not unlike a basket ball ring. Armed with a couple of holding bags I gingerly ascended the

The two Duncan Camerons suffering the predations of midges at the Slog Site.

rungs until I was at eye level with the brood. Surprise number three for the day was a brood of six — almost ready to leave the family seat.

Slowly circling my free arm round the back of the nest I tried to usher the mass of thrashing talons to the near side of the rim, but two took a first flight and floated like parachutists to the floor below. The remainder were bagged and safely brought to earth. The two escapees were easily rounded up and in no time they were ringed. Returning them to the nest took double the time as I carefully placed each one back on the structure, ensuring that my head kept well below the level of the nest. Each time one was released I expected a burst for freedom but they contented themselves with screaming abuse and giving each new occupant a lashing of talons. Despite the racket the hen did not come into the building but when we left she was circling the area.

Next stop was the Silicon Section where once more the security procedure was repeated before we arrived at an open-fronted shed holding barrels of chemicals. This time it was reasonably straightforward. The nest was on a metal 'H' framed beam under the roof and a ladder neatly took us to the spot. All four birds were mobile and took a bit of catching but nothing like the pressure of the previous site. Ringed and photographed they were put back inside my sweater and returned to their very smelly abode. Fifteen down and still an evening sortie to come.

I collected Duncan Cameron a few hours later and we drove into the hills with great confidence. A courtesy visit was made to the new gamekeeper who appreciated the call and didn't object to us ringing the young which was encouraging. It was a long drive along a very dusty hill track until finally the car was parked above a series of earth cliffs. By now I was wary of the number of birds to expect but this time the promised five were all present and correct. Midges hampered the ringing and we were back to the car in no time. The next site was only a short distance further along and Duncan assured me that there were another three young, but this time they were rather well developed. The tree itself, a Scots pine overhanging the stream bed, was a bit of a tester. Although not tall, the stunted trunk was topped by a tangle of branches, and naturally the crow's nest was on the furthest point out over the gully.

I decided to ring the birds in the nest rather than do a double climb and with Duncan's malicious encouragement the nest site was finally reached. True to form the numbers had miraculously increased to five birds, all of which were prepared to have a go. It was a slow business, retrieving each one as they backed off, balancing only with my legs while I ringed, then committing them down my sweater. Twenty-five minutes passed before I was able to climb down, during which Duncan kept up a running commentary on the antics of the irate hen kestrel which showed remarkable boldness in diving at the intruder in the tree.

It always seems a shorter drive home after a successful venture and with 25 kestrels safely ringed I was back in no time.

Towards the end of the ringing period when the pressure to complete the work eases off, you can often indulge in little projects which normally come second in the main stream of timetabling. Never having seen a kestrel brood

All four young safely ringed at the Silicon Plant. Eddie Miller is on the right.

121

bedding down for the night, I decided to join the late shift one evening in late June. The farmer was warned not to worry if the car was at the usual place well into the night. I trudged up the hill at about seven thirty, mentally checking the key items needed for a four to five hour-stint — camera and flash, tripod, black polythene bag for the seat, spare film, some sweets, a drink and, lastly, a torch.

The cock kestrel flew off from one of its favoured perches on the fringe of the sitka plantation but of the hen there was no sign. Fresh droppings at the base of the tree indicated that the birds were still in residence in the old crow's nest. The climb up to the hide platform was achieved on auto pilot and within eight minutes the gear and I were in position. The black bag proved its worth as the seat had become waterlogged due to recent downpours.

Three young, almost ready for fledging, were huddled together staring at the lens. It normally took them about a quarter of an hour to settle down and from then on the hide and its occupants were ignored. A half-consumed pipit lay beside the unhatched egg which somehow had conspired to stay intact despite the daily turmoil in the confined space.

Hardly had I time to take in the scene when the hen landed and dropped a decapitated vole on to the nest and took off almost in the same moment. The hide was totally ignored and I didn't even have time for one exposure from the camera. The vole was mantled by one of the young and, stimulated by the visit, a second chick began to tear at the pipit. Chick number three didn't even raise itself up to a standing position.

Vole and pipit despatched, the birds settled down. Three shuffles to the edge of the nest were the only interruptions for the next hour and a half as white-wash was jettisoned below on to what was rapidly becoming a white sitka spruce. I decided to concentrate on the open hill which was visible from the eyeflap on my right and at about 2115 hrs the cock bird came in and settled on a spruce leader well out of sight of the slumbering young. He preened extensively then settled down close into the trunk and remained statuesque.

By now the overcast sky was contributing to the early darkening and I silently lowered all my gear to the ground so that my exit would be unencumbered. The timing was perfect. No sooner had I climbed back up and settled down again than the hen came directly in and landed on the tree next to the nest. All three young raised themselves up but instead of the normal clamouring they just crouched down again. She didn't have any prey and, just like her mate, proceeded to preen for a good ten minutes. Finally satisfied with her handywork she ruffled the feathers, hunched up and closed her eyes.

By now the visibility was very poor and after half an hour's grace I cautiously exited from the back of the hide. Luckily, she had chosen to roost on the far side of the nest from the hide and the buffer gave me the edge I needed to descend without blowing the whole scene. On saying that, it took a good 15 minutes to negotiate the descent, which at least allowed the blood to course back into starved legs. Time 2310 hrs. Having pinpointed the cock bird I exited the wood well away from his perch and made my way downhill to the car. Not an experience I'd repeat very often.

B.T.O RINGING SCHEME

Much of the information concerning kestrel migration and the turnover of adult populations comes from ringing young in the nest and adults. Being such a potentially damaging operation, ringing is strictly controlled nationally by the British Trust for Ornithology working closely with the Nature Conservancy Council. Bird ringing began in Denmark at the end of the nineteenth century and the British National Scheme's origins can be traced to 1909 when one of two independent operations was launched. H. F. Witterly, the well-known ornithologist, eventually transferred control of his scheme to the B.T.O. in 1937. The Bird Ringing committee which was set up, was chaired by A. Landsborough Thomson, the instigator of the second original enterprise which had been based at Aberdeen University and ended during the First World War.

Today the Scheme operates on a permit system with gradings, from a trainee who is under the 'wing' of an experienced ringer, to an 'A' permit holder, the highest competent level. Enthusiasts pay for the privilege of having a permit. During the course of training the aspiring ringer will be expected to have processed 2,000 to 3,000 birds, both passerines and non-passerines, of at least 50 species. The standards are of necessity very high, as mishandling of birds can easily result in injury, shock and even death.

The ring, which is made of aluminium alloy, is attached to the bird's leg by means of a specially designed pair of pliers and each ring carries a serial number plus the message 'Inform British Museum London SW7'. Once through the training system, the ringer must adhere to the annual paperwork of returning ringing details to the centralised Ringing and Migration Department of the B.T.O. and is rewarded with a computerised form if any of the ringed birds are recovered. Each ringer pays for the rings, though some people have formed ringing groups which buy in bulk, thus cutting down costs. In 1990, 100 kestrel rings – size E cost £16, or £71.50 for 500.

The ringing equipment is not vast and consists of: a finely meshed mist net which can be strung over a large area to catch birds in flight, rings, balances, wing rules and calipers for measuring, and bags for holding the birds.

After their first flights the young familiarise themselves with the area around the nest site.

FLEDGING AND BEYOND

In the last week before the young take their initial flight they have familiarised themselves with the environs of the nest, spending hours standing motionless staring out of the nest. Near fledging, if the site allows, they begin to move out of the nest on to nearby branches and ledges, returning to the safety of the base to feed and roost. They are still very attached to the nest site and return to the nest from the branches and flatten themselves on the nest if alerted by the adults. When an adult comes in with food they call loudly and adopt a begging posture to attract attention. Once the food has been handed over, the adult moves

Recently fledged chick adopting a begging posture when an adult brings in food.

off quickly to avoid the constant badgering. The males leave slightly earlier, at 27–30 days, than the females, 29–32 days, but this is by no means a hard and fast rule.

The fledging period is another of the stress points in the cycle and accidents can happen as inexperienced birds may crash on their initial flight. One bird flew into a pool below the nest and was drowned, while another crashed into a tree and broke one wing. The birds do not all leave at once and very often one bird can be airworthy for days while its nest-mates are still teetering on the brink of the nest. All the strenuous wing exercises practised in the nest or when they were at the 'brancher' stage pay dividends when they take to the air for the first time, often landing clumsily on a nearby tree or banking.

The nesting cliff, wood or building acts as a base initially and one of the most rewarding sights is to see six young kestrels take to the air calling when an adult returns with food. They hang around the nesting area often well spaced out for safety's sake and it's a devil of a job to count exactly how many have fledged. In fact this final piece of information is often very difficult to obtain. The birds are not predictable and may leave the nest at any time within a seven-day period at the end of a cycle. If they are all flying round a wood it is almost impossible to keep track of individual birds to complete an accurate count. Take a typical late season day in the field.

Diary extract – 16 July 1987:

The arrival of the car at the roadside spruce belt signalled a scattering from the wood of blackbirds, mistle thrushes and magpies. The exodus continued as I made may way to the nest tree. Droppings and pellets lay below the tree and I climbed up through heavily white-washed branches. The platform was empty and flattened by the young which were nowhere to be seen. Once down the tree I set out on to the open hill over huge furrows now completely colonised by thistle, buttercup, and grass which all but smothered the young sitka spruce plants. From the brow of the first hill the newly planted ground was scanned and a hen kestrel was soon picked up flying low over the hill pursued by a young bird. They landed on a grassy knoll and, after careful scrutiny, I spotted two more heads.

One hundred metres away the cock bird was trying to hover but the attentions of the last youngster were so disruptive that he made off further into the forest leaving his offspring to settle on a small rock outcrop. Its ring was easily picked out using the binoculars.

Satisfied with the information I drove slowly to the Dam, eyes constantly checking the skyline for family parties of kestrels. The approach to the Dam was uneventful and all that remained at the site were some pellets and recently plucked prey items. The impression was of the site having been vacated for some time and the down clinging to the debris indicated that the single chick had probably survived.

Confirmation came as I reached the car when a young bird broke over the trees calling furiously, and sped towards the hen which had arrived over the quarry with a vole dangling from her talons. The young bird had almost made contact when the hen neatly banked causing the less experienced bird to overshoot badly. This happened twice more before they moved out of range behind the hill. I could still hear the young bird calling but they preferred to practise out of sight.

Back on the road and a final visit to the Magpie Wood. Newly clipped ewes and woolly lambs casually lay by the verges but very few birds were seen. Things improved dramatically at the wood. The calls of the young were audible through the car window as I pulled up on to a grass bank. Moving quietly to the woodland fringe I unfortunately disturbed a young bird from the top of a sitka. Within seconds all six were flying round, calling to each other and coming in to check on the intruder before veering off. It was quite a show. No struggling first flights here. They were now polished performers.

As a matter of efficiency the nest box was checked, but I didn't tarry long as the stench was appalling. White-wash was everywhere, down clung to the branches and the interior was a miniature ploughed field of grey, festering matter. Unfortunately it was impossible to stay and admire the young birds as the midges were unbearable.

The nearby Ram Wood could not have been more different. The wood was quiet but my climb to the nest box alerted the hen which flew over calling loudly. The box was in a similar state to the previous site and it looked like another success story. A quick walk round the perimeter of the wood put up two young but their reaction was to fly quickly into the core of the plantation and settle down. Not a cry was uttered. The presence of the adult and obvious alarm calls had evoked a different reaction from the young which had clamped down. Half an hour's further search was fruitless against the disciplined response of the family.

It is always wise to capitalise on a good run so for the finale I headed down the coast to Kenbain. Ailsa Craig was shrouded in low cloud but a hovering kestrel was a good omen. I parked the car well away from the site and walked in.

The hen took off from her favoured ledge and appeared agitated. Her ragged plumage was obvious as she worked hard to hold station above the cliffline in the blustery conditions. The state of the nest entrance was standard for this time of year, messy, and a quick check revealed the standard fare of debris. I worked my way for half a kilometre along the cliff searching each indentation of the cliff profile without success. Changing strategy, I climbed up on to the cliff top and made my way slowly back. I met the hen again at the nest cliff, still hanging in the air, not 20 metres from where I stood. Oh! for sunshine and a camera. Suddenly it was all action as two of the young came hurtling up the fence line calling loudly and headed straight for the hen. She wisely slipped away and the first young bird followed suit as it saw me. The other bird, thoughts only for its stomach, came straight on until the reality of my presence registered. Panic stricken, it pulled up and only just cleared my head. I could have put out a hand and touched it. What a superb climax to the season.

The young birds gradually drift from the immediate vicinity of the nest site having explored the area thoroughly in the days following their first flight. They then spend at least a month in the company of the adults learning to hunt and survive. Much time is spent hanging around but by the end of the second week out of the nest they are catching insects on the ground. They soon learn to hover but are still very dependent upon the adults for food and respond to an incoming adult by flying unerringly towards them. The adult often plays around before releasing the prey in the air for the young to catch. By the end of the third week the adults have reduced their provision of food for the juveniles thus forcing them to forage much more for themselves. It is not until the end of the fourth week that hover-hunting becomes intense and the first major prey item will be taken. Dispersal from the family group and natal area takes place after six to seven weeks, birds gradually drifting off and becoming independent for the first time.

For me the toil, concentration, and therapy of kestrel fieldwork is over for another season. The kestrel reverts to being a distant figure — the gap rarely bridged until next spring. There is still much paperwork to be attended to — results need to be tabulated, the territory cards brought up to date, ringing details sent off and the season analysed. The story is now taken up from the ringing recoveries which, over the years, have built up into a reasonably detailed picture of the lives of young birds. My next link is the arrival, by post, of the recovery slips from the British Trust for Ornithology Ringing and Migration Section which invariably record the demise of one of the birds I have ringed.

After the break-up of the families, the young birds seem to wander initially in any direction. In the first few months before winter bites, Ayrshire birds have been recorded dead, usually from road accidents, on the Isle of Arran, County Durham, Northern Ireland, South Humberside, Stirling, near Edinburgh, the Isle of May in the Firth of Forth and Dumfriesshire. Several were found dead by the roadside within ten kilometres of their natal site. This random dispersal in the late summer and early autumn has been well-documented by other workers in Britain who have analysed ringing recoveries.

If the young birds from Ayrshire do migrate, then they do so in a wedge, roughly south, south-east. All the recoveries are plotted in Figure 4. The movement can be traced from the south of Scotland to southern England and across the channel to the Continent. Some birds are very quick off the mark. One bird, ringed at Waterhead, reached Humberside by 1 August, another was shot dead in Guernsey at the end of December. Both their records were surpassed. A bird from the Crumbling Quarry territory made it to Holland by 23 October, while another from a different territory reached northern France by 16 November, a distance of 840 kilometres in 150 days. The Continent seems to be well within compass of these migrating juveniles and five birds have been recorded in Spain, Holland and France. A few birds make the short journey to Ireland which seems to be a subsidiary wintering area.

The reason for so much data on juvenile kestrels is quite simple. The mortality rate in the first autumn and winter is extremely high. Sixty-six per cent of Ayrshire ringing recoveries were birds which died before their first breeding

A juvenile kestrel, independent after leaving the family party.

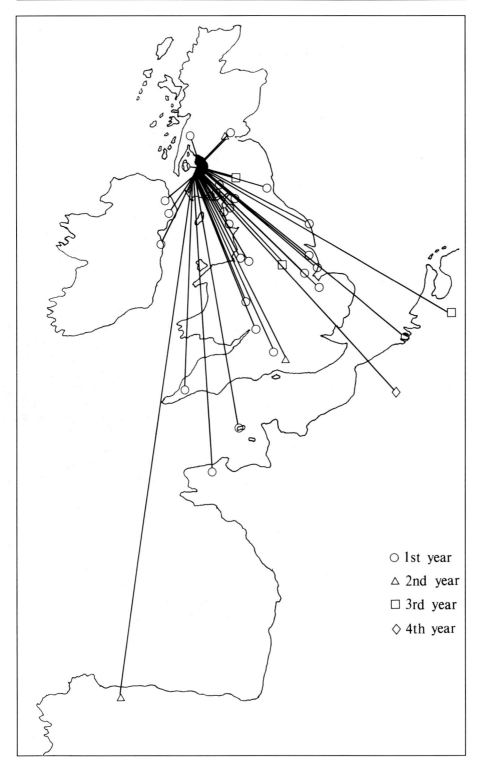

Figure 4
Ringing recovery data
from Ayrshire.

○ 1st year
△ 2nd year
□ 3rd year
◇ 4th year

KESTREL MIGRATION

The kestrel is nomadic by nature so migration is not an unexpected phenomenon. However, putting the Ayrshire data into a national and international context does help to build up a picture of the species' strategy in relation to migration. Put simply, it's all about displacement and food supplies; birds moving out of one region while others move in. Considering conditions in winter in the northern and eastern margins of the kestrel's range, it is hardly surprising that they move out, as the food supply must be extremely limited for a small-mammal hunter in snow and ice regions like Scandinavia.

Prior to the siting of oil installations, a few ringing recoveries hinted at migration of kestrels and some interchange of breeding stocks across the North Sea. The setting up of the North Sea Bird Club and collation of records from oil rigs has confirmed a spring and autumn movement of considerable proportions, assuming that the figures provided are only a percentage of actual numbers. The autumn movement is from Fenno-Scandinavia to Britain.

Juvenile kestrels from Scotland and the north of England move to the south of England and the north fringes of the Continent. On average, juveniles move further south than adults and northern birds further than those of southern England. Ireland is a subsidiary wintering area for kestrels ringed in the north of England and Scotland. Some juveniles from the south of England cross the channel and winter abroad, and the bulk of the recoveries are in France, Belgium and, to a lesser degree, Holland. Ringing recoveries show movement from the Continent of Europe across to Africa and this includes a major trans-Saharan element. Birds have travelled from the Netherlands to Mauritania, Switzerland to Liberia, Czechoslovakia to Ghana and the east of Germany to Nigeria. This last movement completes the displacement process and ensures that the birds are well spaced out. So far no British kestrel has been known to travel to Africa though some birds, born in the south of England, have been recovered in southern Spain.

The main movements of kestrels begin in August on the northern edge of the range and continue throughout September and October in Europe and the southern movement reaches Africa by early October and the equator by the middle of the month. On migration, the kestrels fly higher than when in normal flight and are usually gregarious, being seen in diffuse flocks of several hundred, often mixed with lesser kestrel and redfooted falcons. The return movement begins in southern areas in February and most have left the Tropics by late April. The homeward journey of British birds from Europe begins at the same time with a peak in March. Kestrel migration occurs on wide fronts with concentrations at narrow sea crossings like the Straits of Gibraltar. Peak passages at these bridges occur from mid-August to early November.

season and a third of those did not even survive to the end of September. This figure is very much in line with other British data which has been published.

This high first year mortality is hardly unexpected as the birds will be inexperienced and presumably are unable to provide sufficiently for themselves especially during adverse weather conditions. The November/December period seems to be a particularly vulnerable time when winter conditions begin to cause problems. In one very unusual case, three birds from the same brood at the Dam were all found dead five months later at Market Rasen, Newbury and Barrow-in-Furness. Seven recoveries have occurred from that one territory over the years (Figure 5).

One very interesting trend to emerge from the recoveries was that early hatched young survived better than those which hatched later. The kestrel breeding strategy is aimed at having young in the nest and fledged when food is most plentiful giving the adults the best chance of rearing the brood. Fledging can occur as early as mid-June in Ayrshire and this period coincides with a time when voles are breeding and small bird populations have inexperienced young on the wing. The earlier the birds are fledged, the longer the period they have to gain experience in survival and build up reserves before the onset of winter.

Although only a meagre 26 recoveries have been documented of Ayrshire birds after the first winter, several are of great interest. None of the recoveries in the first breeding season were in Ayrshire, but rather Cornwall, Strangford Lough, Northern Ireland, and a patriotic bird which expired at Bannockburn. Even by the

Young kestrels are particularly vulnerable when winter begins to bite in November and December.

Figure 5
Ringing recoveries from
the Dam Territory.

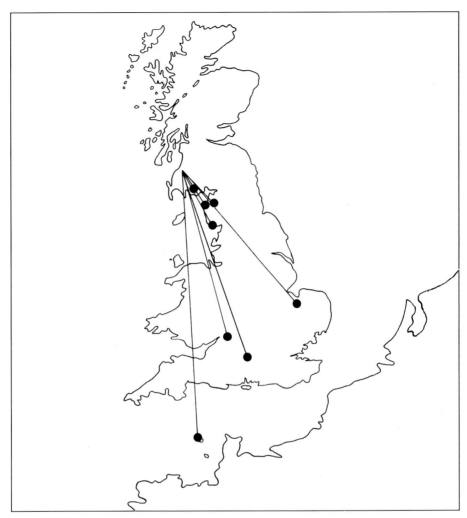

second winter only one out of seven records was in Ayrshire. The Irish connection accounted for two, three were from England, and the furthest travelled Ayrshire kestrel to date, a bird ringed in June 1976 not far from the Dam, hit an electricity pylon in Ovido, Spain 557 days after being ringed, a distance of 1,288 kilometres.

After the second winter the trend changed to home-based recoveries. Of the 14 recoveries only three were outside Ayrshire. Continental winter holidays obviously suited one bird which was killed in north France in its fourth winter. All the records of birds caught or found dead during breeding and after the second breeding season were of birds breeding in the study area — except one. The exception was a three-year-old bird which was killed by a car at Arnhem in May.

I have no records of birds returning to breed at their natal site. The nearest was a hen which bred at the Coastal Cliff in its second year having been reared in an adjacent territory.

The average life span of a kestrel has been calulated at 1.2 or 1.3 years, but some have lived well into their teens. The British record so far is 14 years 5 months but a Swiss bird reached an impressive 17 years. In the study area only three birds are known to have lived to five years or over. A Limekiln youngster ringed in June 1978 was retrapped as a breeding cock bird in the Great Glen territory only 30 kilometres away in 1982. Sadly, it was killed by a car in its fifth winter. One hen bred and was caught each year in the same territory from 1980–85 and she wasn't a first year bird when trapping began. The third bird, a hen, bred for two years in a quarry near Culzean, then was trapped at a tree site four kilometres away and, at the time of writing, is still alive and well having raised two further broods in the same wooded hillside.

Continued ringing of adults and young birds in the same territories in the future will, hopefully, shed more light on this intriguing aspect of the kestrel's lifestyle.

THE TWENTIETH-CENTURY RAPTOR

In the previous nine chapters we have followed a composite breeding season encompassing 18 years and built up a picture of the kestrel's lifestyle. The story would be incomplete without taking a wider perspective on this fascinating bird of prey. What is the kestrel's blueprint not only for survival in an often hostile environment, but also for achieving the status 'common', a feat in itself in the fluctuating world of birds of prey?

Numerically, the estimated 70,000 breeding pairs of kestrels in Britain make up a staggering two-thirds of the total raptor breeding population. Although the sparrowhawk and buzzard outnumber the kestrel in certain localities, this medium-sized falcon is by far the most widespread of Britain's raptors. The kestrel was recorded breeding in over 90 per cent of 10-kilometre squares during the survey for the British Trust for Ornithology Breeding Atlas in the period 1968–72.

Positioned at the top of the food chain, the kestrel has been in the front line whenever major changes or pressures in the environment have occurred and it is fair to say that this resilient bird has flourished while many of its peers have marked time, declined or even become extinct. It is now a symbol of success in a bird world where publicity often equates with rarity or pest status.

There are two main factors in the kestrel's success story, namely the bird's ability as a species to respond positively and quickly to changes in the environment, and its relationship with man. An analysis of certain key elements in the kestrel's lifestyle sheds light on the bird's remarkable ability to change with the times.

The kestrel is a partial migrant and is dispersive by nature. This endemic mobility means that the bird is capable of utilizing favourable conditions such as increased food supply in a district and, allied to reasonable tolerance of near neighbours in a time of plenty, can result in almost colonial breeding at times. Similarly, having such a gypsy-type disposition, the birds are able to exploit suitable feeding areas in winter, unlike some sedentary species, and also search over wide areas in spring for suitable vacant territories.

A high reproductive rate is another essential pre-requisite of this bird's

successful strategy. The essence is a fast turnover of population typical of most middle-sized birds of prey. We have seen that kestrels in general have relatively short lives but this is compensated by the early maturity of youngsters which are capable of breeding in their first year if the opportunity arises. This was brought home to me on one occasion at Kenbain when I was almost fooled by a young cock bird which was still in juvenile plumage. At first I thought I had a classic situation of two hens at one nest but a section of chestnut colour high on the back finally betrayed his sex.

The kestrel is a partial migrant and is dispersive by nature.

Research work in Eskdalemuir has proved the presence of a floating population of non-breeders capable of recruitment into the breeding population if conditions are right – a vacant territory, the loss of one member of a pair during the breeding season, or a time of exceptionally good food supply. There is no reason to suppose that this is not the general situation countrywide. The link with the bird's mobility is extremely important in this context.

The breeding cycle is of reasonably short duration, about four to five months, which means that the birds and young are vulnerable at the nest site for a much shorter period than some of their larger counterparts. The golden eagle's cycle can take up most of the year and they may not even breed annually, the osprey takes nearly 90 days from egg to fledging compared to 60 for the kestrel. If a kestrel clutch is lost at an early stage the cycle can be restarted.

Given good conditions, the birds can lay large clutches and produce large broods as 1988 showed. Clutch sizes averaged 5.4 per pair and of 26 clutches known, no less than eleven had a full clutch of six eggs. Hatching rate was 94 per cent and an average of 3.5 young were reared from all pairs and 4.3 per successful pair. Two years earlier the productive rate of the Ayrshire population had plummetted to an all-time low, due to a consistently cold and wet breeding season when clutch sizes averaged 4.3 and output was only 1.3 young per breeding attempt. This ability to bounce back quickly after a bad season must have been a critical factor in the species' recovery after the traumatic pesticide period. A look at the Ayrshire data in Table 2 shows the variation that can occur in different breeding seasons but, on balance over a long period, the output is very high. A profile of the Dam site on page 139 also illustrates the productivity at a prime territory.

Another great advantage is the lack of specialisation of the kestrel. This may seem a strange statement to make as many people view the kestrel only in terms of a hovering bird of prey. However, take any aspect of its lifestyle and you'll find diversity. The only habitats which exclude kestrels are dense forest and water. The kestrel is at home from coastal strips to the top of the Cairngorms as long as the terrain is open. It is particularly well-adapted to living in urban environments where buildings merely provide surrogate cliffs and the playing fields, parks, gardens and railway lines are good substitutes for rough grassland.

Given good conditions kestrels lay large clutches and produce large broods.

The range of nest sites used by kestrels is equally impressive. Being a cliff nester by nature, it relies heavily on substitutes for ledges but this is no impediment. Buildings of various sorts are used – the Gable End and the

Table 2 **Analysis of annual breeding data 1980–1989, Ayrshire**

	1980	1981	1982	1983	1984	1985	1986	1987	1988	1989
Percentage of territories occupied	74	84	85	64	77	74	58	71	80	77
Percentage of breeding attempts which failed	30	29	33	35	12	29	44	30	17	13
Average clutch size	4·6	5·0	4·7	4·3	5·3	5·2	4·3	5·3	5·4	4·8
Percentage of eggs hatched	68	70	60	70	94	69	50	70	94	82
Average young reared per successful pair	3·3	4·0	3·7	3·0	4·2	3·5	2·2	3·6	4·3	3·8
Average young reared	2·3	2·1	2·4	1·9	3·7	2·5	1·3	2·4	3·5	3·3
Percentage of eggs from which flying young produced	75	58	56	62	83	58	39	52	81	73
Brood survival after hatching (percentage)	90	92	86	90	95	84	74	73	85	86

Limekilns are local examples and the German name *Turmfalke* (Tower Falcon) is testimony to this habit in Central Europe. The old or disused nests of ravens, carrion crows, herons, magpies, sparrowhawks, and holes in trees are equally acceptable.

The bird takes readily to nest boxes as was shown clearly in the Polders in Holland. The introduction of boxes on poles in the low lying agricultural ground, almost devoid of natural nest sites, had the desired effect of increasing the kestrel population dramatically. In one area the numbers of pairs rose from 20 to 109. In my own study plots in Ayrshire, the nest boxes were accepted by kestrels even when alternative crows' nests were available. In fact, kestrels in the neighbouring territories of Ram Wood and the Magpie Wood used nest boxes frequently and were among the most productive pairs in the population.

The role of the carrion crow is critical as, in upland areas where cliff sites are scarce, the crow's stick nests are used regularly by kestrels and merlins. Nearly half the kestrel nests located in upland areas in Ayrshire are in this type of structure. At present, with the decline of gamekeeping on many upland estates, the crow numbers are high and the supply of alternative homes for kestrels would seem to be guaranteed.

In the south-east of England the extensive hurricane damage of 1987, with the loss of thousands of mature deciduous trees, reduced the number of potential

THE DAM – PROFILE AND BREEDING RESULTS 1975–1990

Nest site
behind a ladder in a maintenance platform in the middle of the Dam

Shelter
completely protected from the elements

Disturbance
very little due to inaccessibility – maintenance staff only

Habitat
very mixed – upland heather moor on the fringe, ample rough grassland, mixed woodland and scrub, lochside and river bank

General notes
very productive territory, first noted in 1973. From 1980–89 five different hens bred at the site. Only one failure and one year unoccupied in 15 years. Usually one of the earliest pairs to start breeding in a season.

Year	Clutch	Hatched	Reared	Ringed	Date first egg	Hen
1975	6	5	5	5	20·4	
1976	6	5	5	5	21·4	
1977	6	4	4	0	17·4	
1978	5	5	5	5	22·4	
1979	6	6	6	6	22·4	
1980	5	5	4	4	21·4	A
1981	5	5	5	5	23·4	A
1982	5	4	4	4	5·5	A
1983	4	2	2	2	6·5	B
1984	Not occupied					
1985	6	5	5	5	10·4	C
1986	5	0	deserted		24·4	D
1987	6	3	1	1	24·4	C
1988	5	5	5	5	15·5	D
1989	6	6	6	6	25·4	D
1990	5	4	3	3	17·4	E
Average	5·4	4·3	4			

kestrel nest sites dramatically. Kestrels nest predominantly in holes in trees in this area of the country and nest box schemes are already making up for the depletion of natural sites.

The kestrel will often nest in unusual sites and this unpredictability is also an important factor. In one territory there may be many different sites available to the birds and they will switch around from year to year. Compare this again to large and more predictable species like the osprey and golden eagle which have very traditional sites and are more vulnerable to human persecution. I have spent many spring hours in territories, knowing that kestrels are present but having great difficulty in locating their nest sites.

The subject of food and hunting is a critical one and best illustrates the point about lack of specialisation. Exploiting different prey populations and employing different hunting techniques gives the opportunist kestrel the edge in the survival stakes. The ability to switch from one food source to another when conditions change can mean the difference between surviving the winter or not, or rearing a brood or failing to produce.

In Britain the most intense and comprehensive fieldwork has been targeted at hunting and feeding. Although hunting techniques are broken down into flight hunting and still hunting four different techniques can be identified. Flight hunting, for example, can take two forms. The characteristic hovering or hanging motionless on an updraught is used primarily for hunting small mammals, invertebrates, lizards or frogs. Cruise hunting tends to be used in pursuit of birds or when engaged in piracy from other raptors including its own species. Still hunting is when the bird chooses a favoured perch like a tree, pylon or telegraph pole to survey the immediate vicinity, then drops on prey by means of a shallow glide. Prey is rarely taken in the air but hawking for insects and bats in flight does occur and requires great skill on the part of the kestrel. There is a fascinating account of a kestrel pair co-operating in wearing down a selected long-eared bat which the hen eventually caught.

Kestrels will regularly return to productive areas to hunt and one bird in Dumfriesshire was seen flying repeatedly through cow sheds snatching house sparrows from the floors and rafters. This habit of returning to a good site easily explains the old problem in game rearing pens where, as already mentioned, if the pens are uncovered and the kestrel happens to take one chick, it will return for more.

The kestrel will even feed on the ground and I have watched birds running around in short heather or grass in that shambolic gait catching beetles by the dozen. Following the plough, in the air and on foot, has also been recorded.

So the kestrel has many options, from catching voles on mountain tops up to a height of 1,200 metres to hunting in the littoral zone. Kestrels also maximise the daylight hours and are capable of hunting in very indifferent light. In Ireland, Ushant (France) and the Isle of Man, where voles are absent, the kestrel relies chiefly on the largely nocturnal field mouse, so a good percentage of its work must be crepuscular. The kestrel has also been observed hunting by moonlight and I have observed one bird hunting the verges on a motorway outside Glasgow with the aid of roadside lights, well after dusk.

The range of prey items taken by kestrels is impressive despite unanimous acceptance that the short-tailed field vole is the main bulk prey item of the kestrel in Britain and elsewhere. In Norway, kestrels may not even breed in years when voles are scarce. Other food items are taken according to their relative abundance to voles and their seasonal availability. For example, earthworms are taken when the ground is disturbed by farmwork but only from March to May and in the autumn when ploughing is in progress. In summer, when the earthworms live deeper in the soil, they rarely feature. Birds are taken more in summer when there are plenty of inexperienced juveniles about and in the winter, and frogs are taken in the spring when they are more vulnerable. The pairs nesting in the Dam regularly brought amphibians back to the site in the early part of the season. Lizards have been recorded as prey in early spring when they are prone to basking on bankings blessed with sunshine.

The ability to switch from voles to alternative sources of food was well illustrated in the Ayrshire study plots in 1988 and 1989. In 1988, a year when the voles peaked and were thick on the ground, they were caught in large numbers by the kestrels. The following year saw a predictable crash in the vole population and less than ten per cent of prey items brought into nests under observation consisted of voles. Juvenile pipits, skylarks, starlings and common shrews dominated the menus.

For the final word on kestrels and food I can do no better than refer to a letter which I received from Brian Cosnette who witnessed a cock kestrel feeding on medium-sized black slugs by a roadside. The bird returned regularly to the same perch on a telegraph pole where it concentrated on wiping its bill with its feet, presumably to clean off the slime. Any bird which can sustain itself on the ubiquitous black slug, shunned by most predators, is a winner.

So, mobility and the potential for a fast turnover of the population allied to a lack of specialisation are positive elements in the birds' success story. What is also very impressive is the speed with which this species can react to changes in the environment and its resourcefulness. Urbanisation, triggered by the sudden availability of nest sites and hunting areas in bombed cities, spread quickly and London is a prime example.

In 1898 W. H. Hudson, the well-known ornithologist, commented that it was highly unlikely that kestrels would ever return to London because 'the open spaces in the urban fabric were being built upon'. However, in 1931 a pair nested in a loft of St Paul's School, Hammersmith and by 1950 five pairs were breeding in the sixteen square kilometres of central London. In 1967 the London Natural History Society conducted a survey which revealed that 98 pairs of kestrels were breeding within a 32 kilometre radius of St Paul's Cathedral. A further 13 pairs were probably breeding and 31 pairs possibly breeding.

Today most of our major cities have viable populations. In Birmingham the kestrel breeding numbers began to build up from 1950 to a minimum of 45 territories in 1975. Nesting frequently in commercial and industrial buildings, the nest sites in ventilation shafts and holes in walls were often inaccessible and well-protected by staff who often took a great interest in the proceedings. Food does not seem to be a problem since kestrels are quite adept at removing dining finches, sparrows and blue tits from bird tables.

The treeless Orkney Islands serve up an equally good example of speedy adaptation. In 1945 the late Edward Balfour, RSPB Warden, found a kestrel nesting on the ground in a strip of luxuriant heather having abandoned the traditional cliff site nearby. This was a new departure as kestrel pairs normally nested on the abundant sea cliffs and there was no previous knowledge of ground nests. Two other pairs were suspected of ground nesting nearby that year and follow-up work in subsequent years confirmed a gradual increase in this phenomenon, matched with an increase in the diversity of nest sites used – under low banks, in rabbit burrows, cracks in peaty ground. The common denominator was that they were screened by heather.

By 1955 19 territories had been identified on mainland Orkney and 63 different nest sites had been located including seven in rabbit burrows. Most were in thick heather as opposed to medium or scant foliage. The absence of ground predators on the island meant minimal risk compared to mainland British pairs, and shelduck were their keenest nest site rivals!

In the short space of a decade, kestrels seemed to have abandoned some conventional sites in favour of ground nesting when the advantages of excellent cover and the reduced chance of accidents with young falling out of nests have increased the chances of successful breeding. However, there have been fewer

Hunting on roadside verges can have fatal consequences.

ground-nesting birds reported lately. Ground nesting has rarely been recorded on mainland Britain but Riviere, author of *A History of the Birds of Norfolk*, noted this on several occasions in the Broads in the early part of the century.

The recent exploitation of new hunting grounds is typified by the kestrel hovering over motorway verges though mortality from collisions with cars is an added hazard. Their habit of attending oil installations in the North Sea, sometimes for a few days, and preying on the passage of migrants is yet another recent trend. Real flair! These platforms are ideally placed to provide important island substitutes for kestrels on migration, both for resting and refuelling.

The last piece in the jigsaw is the kestrel's relationship with man. There is little doubt that much of the kestrel's success hinges upon the fact that among raptors it has the enviable position of having virtually no conflicts with traditional countryside practices. In fact, its beneficial role as 'pest controller' was given official recognition along with the barn owl in the Ministry of Agriculture and Fisheries' *Bulletin 140*, published in 1948, where it was described as 'one of the most useful of all birds'.

Even in game preservation circles the kestrel is regarded on the whole as being reasonably harmless and I wonder whether if the bounty system had not been introduced in the nineteenth century, there would have been any pressure on this small falcon. No one can deny that kestrels take some gamebirds, especially in their first few weeks of life, and that a few individuals will return time after time for an easy meal ticket at a rearing pen. However, the weight of evidence does support the view that predation of gamebirds by kestrels is negligible.

The other great bonus for the kestrel is that being common and widespread puts it in the public eye and that very familiarity has bred affection. The kestrel is one of our best known and best loved birds of prey and this manifests itself in all sorts of ways. Kestrels breeding in urban locations are often afforded devoted protection by the people who live or work nearby and woe betide the person who tries to interfere with 'their' birds.

One enterprising pair chose the wing structure of an old Comet aircraft used to train the drivers of air bridges − the extensible tubes which link the terminal building with the door of the aircraft − at Gatwick Airport. During the kestrel's nesting cycle the airport workers refused to disturb them, returning to a normal routine only after the pair had reared five chicks.

Unusual sites chosen by kestrels are regularly featured by the media, for example window boxes in high rise flats and cranes on building sites, and its angular hovering outline has been a delight to sign writers. As a symbol it appears in all sorts of guises − Kestrel Press, Kestrel Marine, Kestrel Tours, on pub signs and, of course, Kestrel Lager. Only the kestrel could have landed such a sponsorship deal.

It was an astute move by someone to choose the kestrel as the symbol for the Young Ornithologists' Club, the junior body of the RSPB, which has a phenomenal membership of over 100,000 children. The appeal of the kestrel, its high profile, and the rapport which the children must feel with their chosen bird must be very encouraging for the future.

THE KESTREL AND THE LAW

The primary legislation affecting wild birds in England, Wales and Scotland is the Wildlife and Countryside Act 1981. The basic premise of the Act is that all wild birds, their nests and eggs are protected by law. Within the Act species are categorised into schedules depending upon their status; for example, rare birds of prey such as the white-tailed eagle and merlin are specially protected by penalties at all times.

The kestrel is protected at all times and must be ringed with a close ring and registered with the Department of the Environment if kept in captivity. A general licence permits the sale of registered birds. It is therefore an offence to take kestrel eggs, poison, trap or shoot kestrels, and remove young from the nest except under licence.

An excellent leaflet interpreting the law is provided by the RSPB (The Lodge, Sandy, Bedfordshire SG19 2DL) called *Wild Birds and the Law* and the *Wildlife and Countryside Act (1981)* can be obtained from Her Majesty's Stationery Office.

Only the kestrel could land such a sponsorship deal.

The sad demise of a young kestrel taken for 'falconry' purposes by children.

Yet there is no room for complacency. Kestrels still die slowly, hanging pathetically from pole traps, are shot at the nest, blasted from the sky or die bewildered in convulsions as poison or pesticides race through their bodies. Children still steal clutches of eggs, and take young for 'falconry' purposes despite the great advances made in the fields of education and protective legislation. Ignorance is still a great enemy. It would indeed be a sad day if the 'windhover' was not a common sight across Britain.

However, the picture is far from bleak. The future of the kestrel will ultimately depend upon how we manage the countryside and also on our collective attitude to the wildlife that lives there. The kestrel population is stable at present and laced with tough individuals which defy generalisations. This fascinating unpredictable opportunist is uniquely equipped to cope with our rapidly changing world and is undeniably the twentieth-century raptor.

APPENDIX 1
STATUS OF THE KESTREL
IN 25 EUROPEAN COUNTRIES

Data on the legal status of the kestrel in Europe is derived from the World Working Group on Birds of Prey Bulletin 1 pp. 58–60 (Meyburg 1983).

Country	Estimated Numbers	Remarks	Source
Britain	70,000	Recovery after pesticide problem; stable at present and close to the level that available habitat could support. Fully protected.	Newton 1984
Spain	30,000	Most numerous raptor after the lesser kestrel; widespread but declining markedly at present possibly due to hunting and toxic chemicals. Fully protected.	Garzon 1977
Poland	10–20,000	Increase after 1945 then stable. Most common raptor in country and possibly on the increase again. Fully protected.	Bijleveld 1974
France	over 10,000	Very widespread at the end of nineteenth century; 50% reduction between 1930 & 1960. Decline has continued in recent years in agricultural regions. Fully protected since 1972. Persecution a problem.	Bijleveld 1974
Italy Sardinia	2–8,000	Stable and viable population but pressure from hunters and taxidermists despite full protection since 1974.	Schenk 1977
Netherlands	4–7,000	Strong population decreased during the early 1960s due to	Fuchs & Gussinklo 1977

		habitat changes affecting prey populations; some recent increases noted. Fully protected.	
Sweden	4,000	Drastic decline to mid 1960s but some recovery following ban on methyl mercury. Fully protected.	Segnestam & Helander 1977
USSR	3,500	Slight increase following full protection. (Population probably much higher than this number which is from Central Russia only). Rapid growth of the carrion crow population has increased the number of potential nest sites.	Galushin 1977
Czechoslovakia	over 3,000	Fully protected but can be taken for falconry purposes. Hunting and pesticides still a problem.	Sladek 1977
Luxemburg	2–2,500	Estimates could be on the high side. Fully protected.	Wassenich 1971
Denmark	2–2,500	Fully protected. Fluctuates but has probably decreased considerably during the last 20 years. Toxic chemicals implicated in the early 1960s.	Dyck et al 1977
Belgium	1,500	The kestrel was the first raptor to be protected in 1956. Severe decline from 1,000 pairs in 1962, 750 pairs in 1975. Some slight increase following this law.	Cramp & Simmons 1980
Finland	500–1,000	Recent dramatic decline from 3–4,000 to less than 500 during 1950–74, the 1962–63 severe winter hitting the populaiton very badly. Fully protected.	Bergman 1977
Bulgaria	100–1,000	Protected. Has been reduced this century. Widespread and most numerous raptor but the population is relatively smaller than that of Central Europe.	Michev 1985 Bijleveld 1977
Hungary	6–700	Population greatly reduced in 1960s but following bans on pesticides has recovered. Breeding success quite good. Fully protected.	Becsy & Keve 1977 Janossy & Haraszthy 1985

| Romania | 240–300 | Decline in some areas, possibly due to habitat changes and chemicals. Fully protected and still the most widespread falcon in the country. | Puscariu & Filipasco 1977 Kalaber 1985 |

The following comments are from countries where the overall numerical data is not known

Yugoslavia		Small stable population, fully protected. Widespread.	Bijleveld 1974
Switzerland		Stable population which shows no signs of declining. Classed as common. Fully protected.	Bijleveld 1974
Portugal		Formerly numerous and widespread but presently at low density and decreasing. Protected.	Fergusson-Lees 1964
Italy (including Sicily & Sardinia)		Sharp decline in the 1960s. 100–1,000 pairs in one 21,000km^2 area in Central Italy. Protected since 1979 but hunters still a major problem.	A & F Petretti 1985 S. Allaven 1980 (Pers comm)
Western Germany		Signs of recent declines in some areas. Protected.	Reichholf 1977
Norway		Widespread but most numerous in south. Becoming increasingly scarce in the north. Declining but no quantitative data. Fully protected.	Bijleveld 1974
Austria		Stable except in built up areas where decreasing. Fully protected.	Bauer 1977
Eastern Germany		Classed with the buzzard as being constant in some areas and slightly declining in others – not acutely endangered. Fully protected.	Bijleveld 1974
Greece		Common – population stable. Protected.	Valigno 1977
Turkey		Widespread but thinly distributed breeding species. Protected. More common on passage and in winter.	Acar, et al 1977.

APPENDIX 2
BIRDS TAKEN AS PREY

(Ayrshire data plus material in current literature)

Teal	*Anas crecca*	Stonechat	*Saxicola torquata*
Grey partridge	*Perdix perdix*	Wheatear	*Oenanthe oenanthe*
Pheasant	*Phasianus colchicus*	Blackbird	*Turdus merula*
Moorhen	*Gallinula chloropus*	Fieldfare	*Turdus pilaris*
Coot	*Fulica atra*	Song thrush	*Turdus philomelos*
Kentish plover	*Charadrius alexandrinus*	Mistle thrush	*Turdus viscivorus*
		Chiffchaff	*Phylloscopus collybita*
Lapwing	*Vanellus vanellus*	Willow warbler	*Phylloscopus trochilus*
Dunlin	*Calidris alpina*	Goldcrest	*Regulus regulus*
Snipe	*Gallinago gallinago*	Bearded tit	*Panurus biarmicus*
Redshank	*Tringa totanus*	Long-tailed tit	*Aegithalos caudatus*
Bartailed godwit	*Limosa lapponica*	Blue tit	*Parus caeruleus*
Common sandpiper	*Actitis hypoleucos*	Great tit	*Parus major*
Turnstone	*Arenaria interpres*	Tree creeper	*Certhia familiaris*
Common tern	*Sterna hirundo*	Jay	*Garrulus glandarius*
Arctic tern	*Sterna paradisaea*	Jackdaw	*Corvus monedula*
Little tern	*Sterna albifrons*	Starling	*Sturnus vulgaris*
Feral pigeon	*Columba livia*	House sparrow	*Passer domesticus*
Wood pigeon	*Columba palumbus*	Tree sparrow	*Passer montanus*
Collared dove	*Streptopelia decaocto*	Chaffinch	*Fringilla coelebs*
Turtle dove	*Streptopelia turtur*	Brambling	*Fringilla montifringilla*
Little owl	*Athene notua*	Greenfinch	*Carduelis chloris*
Swift	*Apus apus*	Goldfinch	*Carduelis carduelis*
Skylark	*Alauda arvensis*	Siskin	*Carduelis spinus*
Meadow pipit	*Anthus pratensis*	Linnet	*Carduelis cannabina*
Rock pipit	*Anthus spinoletta*	Redpoll	*Carduelis flammea*
Pied wagtail	*Motacilla alba*	Bullfinch	*Pyrrhula pyrrhula*
Wren	*Troglodytes troglodytes*	Yellow hammer	*Emberiza citrinella*
Dunnock	*Prunella modularis*	Corn bunting	*Miliaria calandra*
Robin	*Erithacus rubecula*		

APPENDIX 3
MAMMALS TAKEN AS PREY

Mole	*Talpa europaea*
Common shrew	*Sorex araneus*
Pygmy shrew	*Sorex minutus*
Water shrew	*Neomys fodiens*
Noctule bat	*Nyctalus noctula*
Pipistrelle bat	*Pipistrellus pipistrellus*
Long-eared bat	*Plecotus auritus*
Rabbit	*Oryctolagus cuniculus*
Brown hare	*Lepus capensis*
Red squirrel	*Sciurus vulgaris leucourus*
Grey squirrel	*Sciurus carolinensis*
Bank vole	*Clethrionomys glareolus*
Field vole	*Microtus agrestis*
Wood mouse	*Apodemus sylvaticus*
Harvest mouse	*Micromys minutus*
House mouse	*Mus musculus*
Common rat	*Rattus norvegicus*
Weasel	*Mustela nivalis*

APPENDIX 4
NEST SITE REGISTER

A pen picture of the main territories mentioned in the text. The names of territories are fictitious to preserve anonymity and reduce the possibility of undue disturbance.

Coastal Cliff

Typical ledge site on an ivy-covered sea cliff. Plenty of disturbance at the foot of the cliff as the cove is regularly walked, but the site itself needs rope work for access and kestrel pairs have no difficulty rearing young. Mixed farming habitat with ample grassland inland.

Waterhead

One of the territories in the main upland study area. A nest box or carrion crow's nest site is normally used by the kestrels in a small sitka spruce shelter belt. The surrounding area is predominantly upland sheep pasture on the fringe of a large middle-aged forestry plantation. Disturbance is reasonably low, mainly the shepherd and his sheep. Long-eared owls nest in the wood.

Dam

A Scottish Power dam, the nest being located in the inspection tower behind a ladder. Infrequent disturbance due to inaccessibility. Barn owls also use the site. Very varied habitat in the territory, mostly lowland but hill pasture at the periphery.

Limekilns

A variety of nest sites are available at this upland location, the scene of past workings for lime extraction. Two holes in the old building are ideal for kestrels as are several ledges and a raven's nest in the cliffline which had been exposed by the mining operations. Sheep pasture surrounds the sites.

Gable End

An isolated farm steading in a typical upland sheep farm near heather moor. The kestrels use a hole in the gable end of the building. Extensive planting of conifers is in progress and the character of the whole area is changing. Disturbance is high from walkers and the site is vulnerable.

Kenbain

Another coastal cliff with rough pasture making up most of the hinterland. The nest sites favoured are old jackdaw holes in the cliff, an ivy-covered rock face behind wire mesh, hung to prevent rock falls, and a raven's nest.

Magpie Wood
Within sight of Waterhead and similar in composition. Rarely visited except by the shepherd. Used by carrion crows, long-eared owls and a pair of magpies.

The Wells
The fringe of a large semi-mature sitka forest. The kestrel pair nest in old crows' nests near the interface of forest and upland sheep pasture. A very difficult pair to pin down because of the terrain.

Great Glen
A mass of ledges are available on a series of rock faces in a 'U'-shaped glen. Too close to a town and, in recent years, the return of the peregrine has made kestrel breeding attempts infrequent. Sheep pasture on all sides provides good hunting areas.

Quiet Glen
An isolated glen in a well-managed conifer forest. The mature stand of timber supports sparrowhawk and tawny owl as well as kestrels. Limited open grassland may well reduce usage in the future.

Wader Wood
Very similar situation to Waterhead and the Magpie Wood and within the study area. The surrounding area is damp upland grassland ideal for nesting waders. Nest boxes or old crows' nests are used by the kestrels.

Ram Wood
Identical to the Wader, Magpie and Waterhead territories.

Stables
Lowland estate. The birds either nest in one of many holes in the masonry of the ruined stables or in a large hole in the bole of a nearby horse-chestnut tree.

Mallard Wood
A shelter belt of larch, spruce and broadleaves on a lowland farm. The kestrel pair use an old crows' nest in a spruce tree on the edge of the wood. A new rookery is becoming established.

Crumbling Quarry
Nesting on ledges among the jackdaw colony this kestrel pair are relatively safe from children as the rock is in very bad condition and shatters easily. The quarry is on the fringe of upland sheep ground.

The Slog
Two mature Scots pine belts in a sea of middle-aged sitka spruce. The walk in, as the name implies, is lengthy and tedious. Nests are difficult to find and there is very little disturbance.

Lowland Quarry
Medium-sized quarry within easy reach of a town and vulnerable to interference by children. The nest is an old crows' nest behind a gorse bush on the rock face. A mallard usually nests only a couple of yards away.

BIBLIOGRAPHY

Acar, B., Beaman, M. & Porter, R. F. 1977 'Status and migration of birds of prey in Turkey', *Proc. World Conf. Birds of Prey (1975 Vienna)* 182−7.

Adair, P. 1891 and 1893 'The Short-eared Owl and the Kestrel in the Vole Plague districts', *Ann. Scot. Nat. Hist. Soc.* 6: 219−31 and 8:193−202.

Balfour, E. 1955 'Kestrels nesting on the ground in Orkney', *Bird Notes* 26: 245−53.

Bauer, K. 1977 'Present Status of birds of prey in Austria', *Proc. World Conf. Birds of Prey (1975 Vienna)* 83−5.

Baxter, E. V. & Rintoul, L. J. 1953 *The Birds of Scotland* Oliver & Boyd, Edinburgh.

Becsy, L. & Keve, A. 1977 'The Protection and status of birds of prey in Hungary', *Proc. World Conf. Birds of Prey (1975 Vienna)* 125−9.

Bell, R. 1905 *My Strange Pets and Other Memories of Country Life*, Blackwood, Edinburgh.

Bergman, G. 1977 'Birds of prey: The situation in Finland', *Proc. World Conf. Birds of Prey (1975 Vienna)* 91−102.

Bijleveld, M. 1974 *Birds of prey in Europe*, Macmillan, London.

Brown, L. 1976 *Birds of prey; their biology and ecology*, Hamlyn, London.

Brown, L. 1976 *British birds of prey*, Collins, London.

Brown, L. H. & Amadon, D. 1968 *Eagles, Hawks and Falcons of the World*, Country Life Books, London.

Brown, T. 1684 *Of Hawks and Falconry, Tract V*, London.

Cave, A. J. 1968 'The breeding of the Kestrel, *Falco tinnunculus L.* in the reclaimed area Oostelijk Flevoland', *Netherlands J. Zool* 18: 313−407.

Cook, A. S., Bell, A. A. & Haas, M. B. 1982 'Predatory Birds, pesticides and pollution', Cambridge: Institute of Terrestial Ecology.

Cramp, S. 1963 'Toxic chemicals and birds of prey', *British Birds* 56: 124−39.

Cramp, S. & Simmons, K. E. L. (Eds) 1980 *The Birds of the Western Palearctic* Vol. 2, Oxford University Press, Oxford.

Davis, T. A. W. 1975 'Food of the kestrel in winter and early spring', *Bird Study* 22: 85−91.

Davis, T. A. W. 1960 'Kestrel pellets at a winter roost', *British Birds* 53: 281−4.

Dobbs, A. 1982 'Kestrels breeding in Nottinghamshire 1979−1981', *Birds of Nottinghamshire, Ann. Report for 1981* 32−5.

Dyck, J., Edkildsen, J. & Moler, H. S. 1977 'The Status of breeding birds of prey in Denmark 1975', *Proc. World Conf. Birds of Prey (1975 Vienna)* 91−5.

Fairley, J. S. & McLean, A. 1965 'Notes on the summer food of the Kestrel in Northern Ireland', *British Birds* 58: 145−8.

153

Fisher, J. 1966 *The Shell Bird Book*, Ebury Press and Michael Joseph, London.

Fitter, R. S. R. 1949 *London's Birds*, Collins, London.

Fuchs, P. & Fussinklo, J. 1977 'The Status of birds of prey in the Netherlands', *Proc. World Conf. Birds of Prey (1975 Vienna)* 139—43.

Galushin, V. M. 1977 'Recent changes in the actual and legislative status of birds of prey in the USSR', *Proc. World Conf. Birds of Prey (1975 Vienna)* 152—9.

Garzon, J. 1977 'Birds of prey in Spain in the present situation', *Proc. World Conf. Birds of Prey (1975 Vienna)* 159—69.

Gerrard, J. 1986 'Urban nesting Kestrels', *Devon Birds* 39: 3, 62—3.

Glue, D. E. 1971 'Ringing recovery circumstances of small birds of prey', *Bird Study* 18: 137—46.

Glue, D. E. 1986 'Raptor Research Register', *BTO News* 142, Jan—Feb 1986.

Glue, D. E. & Morgan, R. 1977 'Recovery of bird rings in pellets and other prey traces of Owls, Hawks and Falcons', *Bird Study* 24: 111—13.

Gotch, A. F. 1981 *Birds, Their Latin Names Explained*, Blandford Press, Poole.

Graham, G. 1911 'Birds of South Ayrshire', *Trans. Ayr & District Field Club* 1:48 (Kestrel).

Gray, R. 1871 *The Birds of the West of Scotland*, Thomas Murray & Son, Glasgow.

Gray, R. & Anderson, T. 1869 *The Birds of Ayrshire & Wigtownshire*, Thomas Murray & Son, Glasgow.

Greenoak, F. 1979 *All the Birds of the Air — the names, lore and literature of British Birds*, André Deutsch, London.

Griffiths, M. E. 1967 'The population density of the Kestrel in Leicestershire', *Bird Study* 14: 184—90.

Hines, B. 1968 *A Kestrel for a Knave*, Penguin, London.

Holmes, et al, 1957 *Birds of the London Area*, Collins, London.

Janossy, D. & Haraszthy 1985 'The status of birds of prey in Hungary, 1982', *World Work Party on Birds of Prey (IPCB) Bulletin* 2: 44—6.

Jones, C. G., Stiller, F. N & Owadally, A. W. 1981 'An account of the Mauritius Kestrel capture breeding project', *Avicultural Magazine* 87, No: 4: 191—207.

Johns, C. A. 1909 *British Birds in their Haunts*, Routledge, London.

Kalaber, L. 1985 'Status of diurnal birds of prey in Rumania and the problem of their protection', *World Working Party on Birds of Prey (IPCB) Bulletin* 2: 37—43.

Kesteloot, E. J. J. 1977 'Present Situation of birds of prey in Belgium,' *Proc. World Conf. Birds of Prey (1975 Vienna)* 85—7.

Mackie, P. J. 1917 *The Keepers Book*, McCorquodale, Glasgow & London.

Macleod, R. D. 1954 *Key to the Names of British Birds*, Sir Isaac Pitman & Sons, London.

Massa, B. 1977 'The Situation of the Falconifomes in Sicily', *Proc. World Conf. Birds of Prey (1975 Vienna)* 131—2.

McWilliam, J. M. 1936 *The Birds of the Firth of Clyde*, Witherby, London.

Mead, C. J. 1973 'Movements of British Raptors', *Bird Study* 20: 259—84.

Merrett, C. 1667 *Pinax Rerum Naturalium Britannicarum*.

Meyburg, B. U. 1983 *World Working Group on Birds of Prey (IPCB) Bulletin* 1.

Michev, T. 1985 'Status and conservation of raptors in Bulgaria', *World Working Group on Birds of Prey (IPCB) Bulletin* 2: 32—6.

Montier, D. 1968 'A survey of the breeding distribution of the Kestrel, Barn Owl and Tawny Owl in the London area in 1967', *London Bird Report* No: 32: 81—92.

Moreau, R. E. 1972 *The Palaearctic — African bird migration systems*, Academic Press, London.

Newton, I. 1972 'Birds of prey in Scotland, some conservation problems', *Scot Birds* 7: 5—23.

Newton, I. 1984 'Raptors in Britain — a review of the last 150 years', *BTO News* 131: 6—7.

Newton, I. 1979 *Population Ecology of Raptors*, Poyser, Calton.

Newton, I. 1986 *The Sparrowhawk*, Poyser, Calton.

Newton, I., Bell, A A. & Wyllie, I. 1982 'Mortality of Sparrowhawks and Kestrels', *Brit. Birds* 75: 195–204.

O'Conner, R. J. 'Habitat occupancy and regulation of clutch size in the European Kestrel *Falco tinnunculus*', *Bird Study* 29, 1: 17–26.

Parr, D. 1969 'A review of the Status of the Kestrel, Tawny Owl and Barn Owl in Surrey', *Surrey Bird Report 1967* 15: 35–42.

Parslow, J. 1973 *Breeding Birds of Britain and Ireland*, Poyser, Calton.

Paton, E. E. R. & Pike, O. G. 1929 *The Birds of Ayrshire*, Witherby, London.

Paterson, O. M. 1956 'Studies of the breeding biology of the Kestrel *Falco tinnunculus L.* in Copenhagen', *Dansk On. Foren. Tiddske* 50: 134–59 (Danish with English summary).

Pettifer, R. A. 1983 'Seasonal variation, and associated energetic implications in the hunting behaviour of the Kestrel', *Bird Study* 30, 3: 201–6.

Petretti, A. & F. 1985 'Status and conservation of birds of prey in central Italy', *World Working Group on Birds of Prey (ICBP) Bulletin* 2: 67–72.

Prestt, I. 1965 'An enquiry into the recent breeding status of some of the smaller birds of prey and crows in Britain', *Bird Study* 12: 196–221.

Prestt, I. & Bell, A. A. 1966 'An objective method of recording breeding distribution of common birds of prey in Britain', *Bird Study* 13: 277–83.

Puscariu & Filipascu, A. 1977 'The Situation of birds of prey in Rumania 1970–74', *Proc. World Conf. Birds of Prey (1975 Vienna)* 148–52.

Ratcliffe, D. A. 1980 *The Peregrine Falcon*, Poyser, Calton.

Reichholf, J. 1977 'Long-term and seasonal changes in the abundance of the Kestrel', *Anz. orn. Ges Bayern* 16: 191–6.

Richards, G.A. 1966 'A check-list of the birds of Ayrshire', *Ayrshire Archaeological and Natural History Collections* 7: 142 (Kestrel).

Riddle, G. S. 1979 'The Kestrel in Ayrshire 1970–78', *Scot. Birds* 10: 201–15.

Riddle, G. S. 1985 'Kestrels attending oil installations in the North Sea', *North Sea Bird Club Report 1985*. 63–70.

Riddle, G. S. 1986 'The Kestrel on Arran', *The Arran Naturalist* 9: 4–12.

Riddle, G. S. 1987 'Variation in breeding output of Kestrel pairs in Ayrshire 1978–85', *Scot Birds* 14: 138–45.

Roberts, P. J. 1980 'Diet of a Kestrel on Bardsey Island', *Bird Study* 27: 116.

Schenk, H. 1977 'Status and conservation of birds of prey in Sardinia', *Proc. World Conf. Birds of Prey (1975 Vienna)* 132–6.

Segnestam, M. & Helander, B. 1977 'Birds of prey in Sweden', *Proc. World Conf. Birds of Prey (1975 Vienna)* 170–8.

Sharrock, J. T. R. 1976 *The Atlas of Breeding Birds in Britain and Ireland* (BTO/IWC) Poyser, Berkhamstead.

Shrubb, M. 1969 'The present status of the Kestrel in Sussex', *Sussex Bird Report* No: 21: 58–69.

Shrubb, M. 1988 'Farming influences on the food and hunting of Kestrels', *Bird Study* 27: 109–15.

Shrubb, M. 1982 'The hunting behaviour of some farmland Kestrels', *Bird Study* 29:121–8.

Simms, C. 1961 'Indications of the food of the Kestrel in upland districts of Yorkshire', *Bird Study* 8: 148–51.

Simms, C. 1973 'Kestrels nesting close together', *British Birds* 66: 76–7.

Simms, C. 1977 'Kestrels hunting Long-eared Bats', *British Birds* 70. 11: 499–500.

Sladek, J. 1977 'The Status of Birds of Prey in Czechoslovakia', *Proc. World Conf. Birds of Prey (1975 Vienna)* 87–91.

Snow, D. W. 1968 'Movements and mortality of British Kestrels', *Bird Study* 15: 65–83.

Sultana, J. & Gavci, C. 1977 'The Situation of birds of prey in Malta 1975', *Proc. World Conf. Birds of Prey (1975 Vienna)* 136–9.

Swann, H. K. 1913 *A Dictionary of English and Folk Names of British Birds* (repr. 1977), Witherby, London.

Taylor, S. M. 1967 'Breeding Status of the Kestrel', *Proc. Bristol Nat. Soc.* 31–3: 293–6.

Thom, V. M. 1986 *Birds in Scotland* Poyser, Calton.

Thompson, A. L. 1958 'The migrations of British Falcons (Falconidae) as shown by ringing results', *British Birds* 51: 179–88.

Tinburgen, L. 1940 'Beobachtugen uber die Arbeitsteilung des Turmfalken (*Falco tinnunculus*) wahrend der Fortpflanzungszeit', *Ardea* 29: 63–98.

Turner, W. 1544 *Avium precipuarum, quarum apud Plinium et Aristotelem mentio est, brevis et succinta historia.*

Valigno, C. 1977 'The Status of birds of prey in Greece', *Proc. World Conf. Birds of Prey (Vienna 1975)* 118–25.

Village, A. 1990 *The Kestrel*, Poyser, Calton.

Wassenich, V. 1971 'Die Brutvogel Luxemburgs in Zahl und Graphiek', *Regulus* 51: 267–80.

Weir, D. N. 1971 'Mortality of hawks and owls in Speyside', *Bird Study* 18: 147–54.

Willoughby, E. J. & Cade, T. J. 1964 'Breeding behaviour of the American Kestrel (Sparrowhawk)', *Living Bird* 3: 75–96.

Willoughby, F. R. J. 1678 'The Ornithology of Newport Pagnell', *PPB Minet* 1972.

Yalden, D. W. 1980 'Notes on the diet of urban Kestrels', *Bird Study* 27: 235–8.

Yalden, D. W. & Warburton, A. B. 1979 'The diet of the Kestrel in the Lake District', *Bird Study* 26: 163–70.

Yarrell, W. 1871 *A History of British Birds* Vol. 1, John van Voorst, London.

Young, J. G. 1973 'Social nesting and polygamy in Kestrels', *British Birds* 66: 32–3.

INDEX

157